OVER THE EDGE

OVER THE EDGE

JAY JOHNSTONE
and
RICK TALLEY

CONTEMPORARY
BOOKS, INC.
CHICAGO ■ NEW YORK

Library of Congress Cataloging-in-Publication Data

Johnstone, Jay, 1946–
    Over the edge.

    1. Baseball—Anecdotes, facetiae, satire, etc.
I. Talley, Rick.   II. Title.
GV873.J65   1987   796.357'0207   87-5345
ISBN 0-8092-4975-8

Published by Contemporary Books, Inc.
180 North Michigan Avenue, Chicago, Illinois 60601
Manufactured in the United States of America
Library of Congress Catalog Card Number: 87-5345
International Standard Book Number: 0-8092-4975-8

Published simultaneously in Canada by Beaverbooks, Ltd.
195 Allstate Parkway, Valleywood Business Park
Markham, Ontario L3R 4T8 Canada

To my wife, Mary Jayne,
and my mother, Audrey—
and to all the friends who have
helped me make the transition
from baseball to the real world
—Jay Johnstone

CONTENTS

OVER THE EDGE

"

Baseball is a game of more than numbers and dates. It's Al Hrabosky taking a hand grenade into the locker room, Jody Davis splashing a rotten egg on Keith Moreland's chest, Mike Schmidt escaping from sharks, and Gaylord Perry teaching an umpire's son how to throw a spitter.

1
A TRIBUTE TO THE ANTS

I'm writing this book because of the ants.

I know that sounds a little strange, but then so has most of my life.

Back in 1971, for example, I was living in Chicago and one of my White Sox teammates, pitcher Rich Hinton, had a habit of crawling into our apartment through the kitchen window. Sort of like the ants, now that I think about it. But I'm getting ahead of myself.

Anyway, one morning my wife Mary Jayne was standing naked in the kitchen, frying bacon, when Rich came in through the window. They both froze— just stood there, transfixed, until Mary Jayne finally said:

"Good morning, Rich. I'll be right back," and went to put on a robe.

Of course, I was upset. I couldn't believe she burned the bacon.

And that brings me back to the ants.

I was at home in San Marino, California, last spring with both television sets and two radios blaring. I had the Dodgers and the Angels on different TVs inside the house and the same two exhibition games on radios outside.

Why outside? Because I was out there pulling weeds and killing ants—you know, those damned little black ants in long lines that always come back no matter what you do. We had been at war, the ants and I, for a couple of weekends. I'd spray, pour hot water, stomp, yell at them, but I wasn't making much headway.

This particular day I'd duck inside to watch a few pitches every so often, then storm back outside to look for more ants. Then, accidentally, I caught a glimpse of my reflection in the window. There I was, on my hands and knees, bashing the hell out of ants with a shoe. I'm watching my former teammates have a ball at spring training, and I'm pulling weeds and killing ants.

But I got over it—not quite as quickly as Mary Jayne got over the surprise of her morning visitor— but with as little damage.

I'm not really out of baseball, anyhow. Nobody who played in the major leagues for 20 consecutive years is ever "out" of baseball. Baseball is as much a part of my life as those damned ants are a part of my patio.

Yet 1986 was the first year in 30 years that I didn't play competitive baseball. I started with Little League when I was a kid and went on to Pony League, American Legion, high school baseball, the minor leagues, and tours of temporary insanity with the Angels, White Sox, A's, Phillies, Yankees, Padres, Dodgers, Cubs, and Dodgers again.

I got my last major league hit—a game-winner off Montreal's Jeff Reardon—on September 2, 1985, the same day they found the *Titanic*. Dodger manager Tom Lasorda was so happy that he kissed me, which took some of the fun out of the game-winner, but not the memory. Hey, that was just the last of my 1,254 major league hits. I may have gotten the first one on the same day the *Titanic* hit the iceberg. Sometimes it feels that long ago.

Baseball, though, is a game of more than numbers and dates. It is far more than an island in a sea of statistics. It is memories.

And craziness.

It's Al Hrabosky taking a hand grenade into the locker room, Steve Sax breaking Joey Amalfitano's thumb with a low-five handshake, Jody Davis splashing a rotten egg on Keith Moreland's chest, and Orlando Cepeda ducking machine gun bullets in Nicaragua.

It's Mike Schmidt escaping from sharks, Gaylord Perry teaching an umpire's son how to throw a spitter, and Yogi Berra saying about a Steve McQueen movie: "He must have done that one before he died."

It's announcer Jerry Coleman noting that the batter has no balls, Dodger catcher Jack Fimple taking the team bus to the ballpark leaving Lasorda and the rest of the team behind, and sportswriter Peter Schmuck putting a crab in Donnie Moore's bed.

It's Lasorda undressing on the pitcher's mound.

It's hitting home runs for nuns, catching bras and panties thrown from bleacher fans, and winning games because your shoes were shined.

It's Old-Timers Games, the College World Series, revolutions in Central America, and Davey Johnson getting benched by the Tokyo Giants because he missed a few swings in batting practice.

It's going over the edge.

I miss Jerry Reuss. If he isn't over the edge, he's somewhere nearby. As well as being a powerful pitcher for the Dodgers during the early 1980s (58–32 over four seasons), he was also one of my running mates. And he's tops at dragging infields.

Perhaps Jerry's *coup de grace* came during the 1986 season, after I had already been relegated to killing ants.

The Dodgers were in Chicago in early May to play the Cubs and it was one of those rare occasions when the White Sox were also at home, playing the Yankees. After the Dodgers' afternoon game at Wrigley Field, Reuss and teammate Rick Honeycutt decided to taxi down to Comiskey Park to watch the Chisox and Yankees.

But watching wasn't enough for Reuss, the man who once conned rookies into delivering sperm samples to the Dodgertown nurse. He had packed towels into his equipment bag, and he and Honeycutt talked their way past the guard outside the Yankee clubhouse.

"I've been traded to the Yankees," said Reuss to the guard.

It was a plausible tale because Reuss's name had been mentioned in trade rumors involving New York. The guard bought it.

Inside, Reuss didn't hesitate. He walked through the clubhouse waving to players he knew and saying, "Pleased to meet you" to those he didn't. Then he went straight to new manager Lou Piniella's office, dropped his equipment bag on the desk, reached out his hand and said, "Hi, Lou. I'm Jerry Reuss."

"I know who you are," said the puzzled Piniella. "But what are you doing here?"

"Didn't you hear? The deal went through."

"What deal?"

"I'm your new pitcher. Didn't George call you? Maybe we should close the door."

"Yeah, maybe we should," said Piniella, who got up and closed the door.

"I haven't pitched since Friday," said Reuss, "but I'll do whatever you want me to do."

"Nobody told me anything!" said Piniella. "What's going on?"

Reuss, with one of his sneaky smiles, then said:

"Here. Open my equipment bag."

Piniella did, saw the towels, and realized how firmly he'd been hooked.

"He really had me," Piniella later admitted. "Hey, with this team it could have happened."

Reuss then walked out of the clubhouse without saying another word to any of the Yankees, watched five innings, and returned with Honeycutt to the Dodgers' hotel.

Jerry's post-prank comment: "Hey, if I have to suffer through all those rumors, can't I have some fun, too?"

Reuss is the same deviant who last season asked outfielder Kenny Landreaux if he could borrow four wristbands.

Landreaux complied, reaching into his sack of wristbands and handing Jerry a package.

"But there are only two wristbands in the package," said Reuss. "I need four."

Landreaux then handed him another package, which had already been opened, and it contained only one wristband.

"Now I have only three," said Reuss. "I need four.

Here, K.T., I'll give you the package with one and you give me another package with two. Then I'll have four."

By now, Landreaux was starting to get confused, but being a friendly sort, he made the exchange. Then he looked at the single wristband and said:

"I wonder who took the other one?"

'I did," said Jack Fimple, from a nearby locker.

"But that leaves you with one extra wristband for the right hand," said Reuss to Landreaux.

"Huh?" said Landreaux, now completely bewildered.

"Not only that," chimed in Kenny Howell. "You gave Reuss right-handed wristbands and he's left-handed."

"How can you tell?"

"Just look at them," said Howell. "Can't you tell the difference between right-handed and left-handed wristbands?"

Reuss then gave back two of the wristbands in mock disgust and the puzzled Landreaux put them back into the sack. Just then, somebody else came over and said:

"Hey, I'll take those if you're giving them away."

"Sorry," said K.T., "you're left-handed and all I've got left are these right-handed ones."

That's my guy, Reuss. When I played with the Dodgers in 1985, Jerry pulled off one of the most amazing pranks I've ever seen. You might call it coincidence but, knowing Jerry, I'm not so sure. He has some weird connections.

It started on a blistering day at Dodger Stadium. Frank Pulli was umpiring home plate and Reuss, compassionate man that he is, sent the ballboy out between innings with a drink. But Reuss didn't send the cold water Pulli expected. He sent hot coffee.

Then Reuss snuck a new baseball out of the ump's ballbag—one that was rubbed up and ready for play—and inscribed it with ballpoint pen: "To Frank, May God Bless You—Tom Lasorda." He returned the ball to the bag and waited to see Frank's surprise when he pulled out the ball.

But Reuss got no satisfaction. Pulli either didn't put the ball into play or didn't notice the message when he did.

Later in the clubhouse, relief pitcher Tom Niedenfuer sat next to Reuss and said: "Damnedest thing happened out there. I'm pitching in the ninth inning, I look down at the baseball and it's got some kind of message written on it."

"Oh, really?" said the delighted Reuss. "What did you do with it?"

"I threw it. I wasn't going to pass up a chance to throw a ball that had been marked."

"And then what happened?"

"Nothing," said Niedenfuer. "It got fouled off."

But that's not the end of the story. The ball had been fouled back into the section where Lasorda's wife, Jo, was sitting, and a man caught it. The guy read the inscription and, boy, was he impressed. Not only did he have a souvenir signed by the manager, it was personalized.

The man's name was Frank.

Nice going, Jerry Reuss. Remind me to invite you to my next seance.

And that baseball should be sent to Cooperstown via satellite.

Some of the best pranks are the sly ones. That Katzenjammer stuff is OK—I enjoy putting hot salve in someone's undershorts as much as the next guy, just as long as I don't get caught—but a sly move shows a touch of class.

That's why Gene Autry is in my Hall of Fame.

Autry, the 80-year-old owner of the California Angels, deserves to see his baseball team in the World Series more than any owner in baseball. As all baseball fans know, he was one pitch away last October during Game Five of the American League playoffs, when Dave Henderson of the Boston Red Sox hit that 2–2 pitch off Donnie Moore into the Anaheim Stadium seats. But that's another story. Having once played with the Angels, I suppose I want so badly to see them succeed. Let's get back, though, to Autry, that sly, singing cowboy.

The scene was the winter baseball meetings in Houston, Texas, a few years ago, in the private dining room of a fine restaurant. The Angels were entertaining their coaches, front office personnel, and members of the media.

Autry sat at a circular table between two of his longtime buddies, then–publicity director Red Patterson and Los Angeles sportswriter Bob "Chopper" Hunter. Both in their seventies, Patterson and Hunter have shared many evenings and more than a few cocktails with Autry since he purchased the Angels over 25 years ago. They are true pals.

Mrs. Autry—Gene's second wife, Jackie—was sitting nearby at another table. Concerned that the Cowboy might be drinking something stronger than iced tea, Jackie kept glancing at his table. The good ol' boys were laughing and enjoying themselves so much, in fact, that Jackie got suspicious. She got up, walked to her husband's shoulder, and looked down.

"Don't worry, honey," said Gene, with the smile of

an innocent man. "I'm not drinking."

With that, she reached down, took his drink, and sipped from it. Satisfied that it was water, she returned to her guests at the other table.

Afterward, one guest—aghast at Mrs. Autry's behavior—cornered Hunter. "It was embarrassing to watch her taste his drink like he was a child," said the offended guest.

"No problem," said Chopper. "She went for the decoy."

"The what?"

"The 'deke.' Gene had a vodka on the rocks in front of me and one in front of Patterson. He kept water in front of him as a decoy and she went for it."

My kind of guy.

Back in the clubhouse, though, humor returns to the basics—even at Wrigley Field, where there hasn't been much to laugh about lately except the Cubs.

Jody Davis and Keith Moreland, a couple of my ex-teammates from the 1984 division champions, were the principals in one particularly smelly incident.

It started when Bill Claussen, the Cubs' strength coach, took a group into the weight room for a series of bench presses. To make things more interesting, Claussen also took along a dozen eggs. He would place an egg on the chest of a flat-on-his-back player doing bench presses. Objective: Six bench presses, each time bringing the bar down to the egg and back up again.

As soon as Terry Francona finished his six, Davis reached down and tried to smash the egg. It was hard-boiled, though, so there was no damage.

Then it was Moreland's turn, and after his fifth "rip," the bar came down on top of the egg, which went splat. Everybody laughed, but that wasn't enough for Jody. He reached over and smashed the egg all over Moreland's chest.

There was only one problem. Not only was this egg not hard-boiled, it was rotten. When the stench hit the weight room, 10 guys ran for cover.

"Grossest thing I ever smelled in my life," said Davis. "And it was all over Zonk's chest. I had a batting glove on my hand and had to throw it into the trash can. We started spraying Right Guard over everything. We even lit matches. Nothing worked."

Moreland, meanwhile, was racing into the shower, gagging and holding his nose, while stripping off his clothes under the water.

"It was the raunchiest thing I have ever smelled in my life," said Davis.

And I'm wondering if ants can smell.

By now you're probably getting a hint about the contents of this book.

The game of baseball hasn't changed, but I can't say that about the players. *They* have changed. There's an old cliché that, to be successful, a ballplayer must be smart enough to play the game and dumb enough to think it matters.

I've never agreed with that. It doesn't take a lot of brains to play baseball, and caring about winning and losing isn't dumb. Winning and losing is what everybody does every day. It's what stockbrokers and car salesmen and ant-killers do.

It isn't winning or losing that's difficult, anyhow. It's *coping* with the winning and losing—keeping it in perspective—and that's where the laughter and craziness come into play.

That's why Charlie Kerfeld of the Houston Astros

will be just fine. He came racing behind third base to back up a play at Dodger Stadium a couple of years ago, turned to the Dodger dugout, and said, "Anybody got a six-pack?" Charlie has reduced his beer consumption (and his waistline) since, but he still owns his wardrobe of Jetson T-shirts and sometimes I wonder if he's one of the few characters left in the game.

Not that there aren't closet kooks out there. It's just that they're more restricted than they used to be. They don't room together, hang together, or sit on planes together—their contracts provide that they sit next to an empty seat. They're making more money now, too—but hey, Jerry Reuss was making $1 million a year the last time I looked, and he still wants to drag the infield again.

It was really great to see nice guys like Wally Joyner and Steve Sax have tremendous seasons in 1986. Joyner could have been Rookie of the Year in the AL and Sax, with just a little earlier start, might have won the NL batting title.

I'd feel better about both of them, though, if they'd lock their managers in their rooms sometime this season. On second thought, perhaps that wouldn't be such a good idea with Mauch. He might jump out a window. But you wouldn't have to worry about Lasorda. He wouldn't fit.

Over the edge we go, then, into this second book written by John William Johnstone, Jr., a.k.a. Crazy Jay. It's giving me something to do other than kill ants.

There will be nothing in this book, incidentally, about putting a brownie into Steve Garvey's glove, cutting down Ron Cey's locker to real penguin size, rooming with Jim Piersall, or playing Green Hornet pranks at Dodgertown. I chronicled *those* adventures in *Temporary Insanity*, discovering afterward what I already suspected: that I wasn't the only cuckoo flying around Peter Ueberroth's nest. Other players, retired and current, started coming up to me and saying "Hey, Jay, I always knew you were goofy but did you hear about . . ."

You'll hear about all sorts of foolishness here, including some more about John William Johnstone, Jr.—gardener, auto parts dealer, broadcasting personality, actor, baseball critic, author, and general, all-around entrepreneur.

Did you hear about the time Yankee manager Lou Piniella asked umpire Marty Springstead, "Where the fuck was that pitch at?"

"Don't you know," replied Springstead, stepping in front of the batter's box and deliberately taking extra time while dusting off the plate, "that you're not supposed to end a sentence with a preposition?"

"OK," roared Piniella, "Where the fuck was that pitch at, you asshole?"

Welcome to the Theater of Baseball Bizarre.

❝

Dodger mangement cited the 'objectional language' on pages 99 and 100 of *Temporary Insanity* as justification for banning my book. My parents weren't very happy, either. My mom gave somebody an autographed copy but tore out page 99. My dad just gave me one of his stern looks and said, 'You shouldn't have used those words.'

2
CONFESSIONS
OF AN AUTHOR

Banned.

I couldn't believe it. There on my breakfast table was the headline from the August 31, 1985, edition of the *Los Angeles Times* sports section:

"Johnstone Book Banned at Stadium's Stands."

The stadium was Dodger Stadium, home of my employer at the time, the Los Angeles Dodgers. And my first book, *Temporary Insanity,* had been banned from sale at Dodger Stadium novelty stands, while such classics as *The Artful Dodger* by Tom Lasorda and *The Dodger Way to Play Baseball* by Al Campanis could still be purchased.

Why? Why me?

Was it because I wasn't hitting? Was I having an affair with the groundskeeper's wife or the publicity director's secretary? Was it because my book was selling so well?

Or was I finally being nailed for using the manager's telephone?

It was none of that. It was a matter of taste.

Dodger management cited the "objectionable language" on pages 99 and 100 of *Temporary Insanity* as justification for banning my book. Actually, it wasn't an obscene book at all, unless Dodger censors consider Larry Bowa beating up a toilet bowl with his bat dirty.

The Dodgers objected particularly to a passage that contained 44 expletives from a verbatim clubhouse speech made by Lee Elia when he managed the Chicago Cubs in 1983.

There were 36 *fuckin's*, two *shits*, four *motherfuckers*, and two *cocksuckers* in his speech, and he didn't even need a deep breath.

"We don't think that is something we should be selling at Dodger Stadium," said Fred Claire, executive vice president. "It didn't seem the proper thing. In our judgment, we don't think it fits our style of the promotion of baseball."

I was crushed. The book contained hardly any other profanity—and, believe me, it took considerable editing to get Lasorda into print—yet it was being *banned!*

All I wanted to do by printing Elia's speech was (a) show how loyal he was to his players by lashing out at the press and taking all of the heat, (b) accurately show how baseball managers often talk, and (c) fill page 99.

Instead, I had a dirty book on my hands and off the shelves at Dodger Stadium.

Even Elia, who had since been fired by the Cubs, reacted. "Now that's what I'll be remembered for in baseball," said Lee, who was right. "Besides, you didn't even send me a copy of the book. And could you give me the business card of the guy who helped you write it? I might want to write one of my own."

Then there was a friend's minister who quoted from *Temporary Insanity* in his Sunday sermon.

"You've got to be kidding," I said.

"He quoted from just parts of it, Jay," said my friend. "Not page 99."

My parents weren't very happy, either. My mom gave somebody an autographed copy but tore out page 99 before she delivered it. My dad just gave me one of his stern looks and said, "You shouldn't have used those words."

Maybe he's right. I wasn't trying to shock anybody or sell more books with page 99. Ballplayers are so accustomed to such language that I never gave it a second thought. Clubhouses are not that much different in usage and speech patterns than military barracks.

But I can understand the Dodgers' point of view. Ballplayers are held up as role models for young boys, as they should be. Fathers who buy baseball books for their sons don't want to admit that their sons already know such words exist.

Therefore, I promised my mother I wouldn't include such explicit language in this second book, except on the rare occasion when it would make no sense to change it.

There will, however, be a page 99 for those who want realism. I'll leave it blank and you can create your own clubhouse situation—how about Gene Mauch discussing pitch selection with Donnie Moore or Bill Buckner talking with the press about the art of bending over?—or fill in the blank page with your own clubhouse speech, using any words you feel might be appropriate.

As for me, I learned my lesson in publishing. You

won't catch me getting banned again. There will be very little use in this book of that often-used-in-baseball word which, incidentally, was derived from the Old English usage, "Fornication Under Consent of the King."

Consent of the king is one thing—but if you're going to talk like that at Dodger Stadium, you need consent of Mr. O'Malley.

Ergo, a new word! *Fuco'm.*

I should have known there would be problems with *Temporary Insanity* when the photographer scheduled to shoot the book cover broke his leg.

Actually, he broke it before reaching the assignment in Vero Beach, Florida.

Actually, he broke it on the way.

Actually, he broke it when he stepped off a curb in Chicago, en route to O'Hare Airport, and got hit by a taxi.

But instead of going to a doctor or hospital, this enterprising artist got on the plane anyhow. He didn't know his leg was broken. When you live in Chicago, it's hard to tell sometimes. He just figured the leg was bruised and hurt because it was so damned cold.

By the time he reached Florida, his leg was swollen and the guy was a mess. I found him in the Dodgertown parking lot, moaning in the back seat of a rental car. The first thing he asked was when I could be in uniform, ready to pose.

That's either dedication or stupidity. I voted for stupidity and sent him off to the Indian River Hospital. But the guy just wouldn't give up: he wanted to rig his cameras and strobe lights and shoot the cover in his hospital room. But I felt a little strange posing for a photographer, with his leg in a hoist. So we left him hanging, hired a freelance photographer, and shot the cover—with me wearing a straitjacket—in the back room of the Dodgertown infirmary. Yes, just a few feet from where I once substituted apple juice for urine and chug-a-lugged it in front of a mortified nurse.

Shooting the cover was a piece of cake. Anybody can look crazy wearing a straitjacket and holding a baseball bat. I've known lots of guys who can look crazy just holding a bat. But I had already made the most important decision involving *Temporary Insanity*, anyhow. My conversation with my wonderful editor, Shari Lesser Wenk, involving that momentous decision had gone like this:

"Before we go any further," she had said, "is there anything about this book that concerns you?"

"Yes," I said. "The color. I'm very concerned about the color."

"What?" she blinked.

"The color. I want it to be a bright color, like maybe shiny yellow or blue."

"Are you kidding?" I guess she had heard about me.

"No, I'm not kidding. I want my book cover to be a bright color so that when people go into a bookstore they'll notice it and buy it."

She tried to assure me that the contents of the book were pretty important, too, but I was relentless.

"Haven't you ever heard that people judge books by their covers?" I said.

"This is a first," she mumbled. "The guy doesn't care what goes into the book but he wants a bright cover."

So she gave me a bright blue cover with large yellow letters and I'm convinced that's why *Tempo-*

rary Insanity ranked fourth in hardcover sales for sports books in 1985, behind bestsellers by Howard Cosell, Mickey Mantle, and Bob Hope (which actually wasn't a sports book, anyhow). And I'm sure the others would have sold more if their covers had been brighter.

One other tip about writing a bestselling book, just in case you're considering it: the title is important. Baseball writer Gordon Verrell of the *Long Beach Press-Telegram*, for example, will certainly have a winner if he ever finishes (or starts) his autobiography: *The Bags Were Loaded and So Was I*. And John Kerr, former NBA great and now radio-TV announcer with the Chicago Bulls, always said his book title should be *Ten Years in the Pivot Without the Ball.*

Picking the title for this second book, *Over the Edge*, was a snap, at least for my editor, who insists that over the edge is precisely where I put her. But I prefer to look at it this way: Here I am, no longer a ballplayer, wondering where the first 39 years of my life went (breaking ball, low and away?). So I posed for this cover at Wrigley Field, where some of the craziest plays in baseball history have occurred— without being posed.

Modestly, I must say that I have been very cooperative with my editor. No prima donna here. That's why I can't understand why she's always screaming at me and telling me how I'm ruining her life.

She really should do something about that.

When you write a book, too, you must be prepared for reaction and criticism. I was lucky. Jim Murray of the *Los Angeles Times* suggested that I had a "nice eye for the lunacy of the grand old game, of which there's a lot. Where there wasn't any, Jay introduced it."

Then there was a column by John Hall of the *Orange County Register* suggesting that, in addition to being funny, I had also enjoyed a career of winning, pointing out that when I was with the 1981 Dodgers they won the World Series, when I was a Yankee in 1978 they won the World Series, when I was with the Phillies in 1976 and 1977 they won pennants, when I was with the Cubs in 1984 they reached the playoffs for the first time in 39 years and, back with the Dodgers again in 1985, we won the division only to lose in the playoffs to St. Louis on Jack Clark's home run.

That was nice of John, but I would be the last to claim my presence transformed those teams into winners. What Hall was suggesting was that laughter is conducive to winning and that I had helped in the giggle department.

"I've got this secret theory about Jay," writer Hall said to Dodger manager Lasorda one day.

"You've got a theory?" answered Lasorda. "What do you think I've got? I've got a headache!"

All reviews weren't raves. One writer, Bill McClellan of the *St. Louis Post-Dispatch*, suggested that the book title described the state of mind of anybody who would buy it.

I liked that because it helped explain why the book sold so well. There are lots of sick people out there who like bright covers.

Probably the best line offered regarding the marriage of my first book and my last season as an active player came from writer Bob Hunter of the *Los Angeles Daily News*. I spent most of the 1985 season on the disabled list (due to a hip inflammation caused by stepping on a sprinkler head in the outfield), so I didn't get my second base hit for the Dodgers until that 11th-inning game winner off Jeff Reardon of Montreal in early September.

"Now Johnstone has three hits this season," said Chopper, "counting his book."

Oh, another thing about that hit, which was also my last in the major leagues. The next day I was walking past Expo manager Bob "Buck" Rodgers behind the Dodger Stadium batting cage. He's my friend, right? Here's a guy I played with for five years with the Angels so you'd think I'd get at least one "attaboy."

But Rodgers is a *big league manager* now and managers live in a different world. After all, he could have walked me the night before with first base open. He knew, though, that I hadn't batted since the Fourth of July and hadn't gotten a hit since April 14, so he figured the odds were in Reardon's favor—about 1,000 to 1.

Maybe he even guessed that when coach Monty Basgall turned to me in the dugout (I was the only player left on the bench), he said: "You can't hide any longer, Jay. It's up to you."

So I worked Reardon to 1 and 1, stuck out the bat to connect with a down-and-in fastball, and plunked a soft liner about 10 feet in front of outfielder Andre Dawson, who didn't even bother picking it up as the winning run scored.

Now it's the next day and all Buck Rodgers says to me as I walk past is, "Fuck you." That made me feel better. I had worried that Buck had forgotten what good friends we were.

One last thing about the reaction to *Temporary*

Insanity: the fans were great. After the book was banned at Dodger Stadium, I simply had a few cases of books delivered to the clubhouse to store in my locker. Then, dressed in uniform, I would wander through the stands before a game and sell them at a discounted price. The fans loved it and I probably sold more than the novelty shops would have sold, anyhow.

There were letters, too. Frank Sinatra sent one, as did President Reagan and Reverend Robert Schuller. There was a warm note, too, from Los Angeles Mayor Tom Bradley, who said he enjoyed reading my book so much on a cross-country plane trip that he forgot to prepare his speech. I later asked him if he wanted to hire me as a speech writer, but he coughed and changed the subject.

One fan, artist Stephen Bentley of Monrovia, California, sent along a caricature of me getting hit in the face with a pie, but Dodger vice president Al Campanis went one step farther. Before a game at Wrigley Field, he unloaded a shaving cream pie into my face, then walked away saying, "I've always wanted to do that."

My favorite fan letter, though, came from a young man from Lynnfield, Massachusetts, who had either purchased, borrowed, or stolen *Temporary Insanity*. This is his letter:

Dear Jay,
    I'm 15 years old and live in Massachusetts. First, I'd like to say that I read your book and it was the best damn book I've read in my life. Since I read your book, I think you should read my letter.
    Let's get one thing straight off the bat: your book was uncensored—so is my letter. By the way, my name is Daryl Brilliant. Me and my best friend Andy

Carbone are just like you except we go a little light on the pranks.

Still reading? Good. We aren't a couple of hot-shit athletes who have Reggie Jackson egos, but we've been following baseball all of our lives. I'm not saying we stink at baseball, but we aren't superstars.

I loved your All-Crazy Team, and me and Andy have something similar, our All-Classic Team. I can comprehend your going nuts over that lost Star Patrol helmet. I have a cousin who had one but I don't know if he still has it. If he does I'll send it to you.

Well, moving on, this summer has been OK—having homerun contests and playing computer baseball with real players and stats. Here is my schedule: 12 hours of sleep, 12 hours of TV, and 12 hours of baseball.

My biggest two thrills with major leaguers were, first, having a conversation with Dave Stapleton over lunch about why he doesn't get more playing time (the next week we asked John McNamara why Stapleton doesn't play more and he gave us a great comeback of "If it was any of your damn business, you'd be the first to know!"). Second, was going to a Bosox game against the Angels. Reggie Jackson was floating around on his ego after hitting two HRs the previous night (if I could get to where he was I wouldn't be any different than him). He walked around the field making people chant "Reggie," but gloatingly wouldn't sign any autographs. Everyone was desperately shoving pens and items in his direction. I even had a 1981 baseball card of him that said "Reggie Jackson, Mr. Baseball." He looked at it and since it was drizzling, took it and wiped it on his leg while walking to the dugout.

Then me and Andy went NUTS! He started showing it to Doug Corbett, Robby Wilfong, Bob Clear, and others. Then he took it down into the locker room. Minutes later, he came up, gave it back to me, and signed it.

I think anybody who can make it into the big leagues is great, and here is my All-Classic Team.

[Editor's note: Mr Brilliant's team is included among other Jay Johnstone lists in Chapter 12.]

Are you still reading? Good.

Well, finally, no letter is complete without asking you for an autograph. Please sign my card "To Daryl" and sign Andy's "To Andy."

Well, if you're ever in Lynnfield, Massachusetts, just feel free to drop by.

Thank you very much. Your lifelong follower,

Daryl Brilliant

There you have it, anatomy of a first book. For a while, I carried Daryl's pasted-up baseball card in my wallet next to my old Marine I.D. card. I figured the kid might make it big someday and the autograph would be worth something.

In the meantime, there's probably some beleaguered high school coach up in Lynnfield, Massachusetts, who's wondering which smart aleck on the team has been spiking the Gatorade and pasting the scorebook sheets together.

Attaboy, Daryl.

You've never been in a light bulb fight? We'd go to neighborhood grade schools, unscrew light bulbs, and run along rooftops, jumping from building to building, throwing missiles at each other. You'd hear a 'pop' and the stuff would be flying all over the place.

3
SO MAYBE IT WASN'T TEMPORARY

I'm not sure when or where I first went over the edge. Who keeps track of things like that? It may have been during one of my football games at Edgewood High School in West Covina, California. We were pretty good—conference champions, in fact—but I drove our coach, Ken Wells, bananas. He would send in plays and I would change them. It agitated him considerably but what was he going to do? I was a pretty good quarterback and gained more than 1,000 yards my senior year.

One night coach Wells announced at a pregame meeting that we were going to try a new game plan.

"What is it?" I asked.

"Give the ball to Jay," he said, "and everybody else get out of the way." And he walked out.

I guess I also skipped along the edge when we played cemetery tag—sort of a 1960s, *American Graffiti* version of hide-and-seek—near an old mansion in nearby Pomona. It was a small cemetery, but when it's pitch dark and you're a teenager, you don't need a big cemetery.

Our idea of fun was to slip through the barbed wire into the cemetery at night and try to get past the caretaker at the three-story, circa 1875 Phillips Mansion without getting caught.

The caretaker was an old guy but he had a big dog and a shotgun that he wasn't afraid to fire into the darkness. Maybe the guy was nervous because of the mansion's resident ghost, who, we had heard, snored at night.

Anyhow, there was some risk. Once inside the grounds and into the Spadra Cemetery, we'd form teams and challenge each other by playing tag between the tombs, hiding and chasing through the shadows, hoping to keep from ripping our shirts on the barbed wire or getting a seatful of buckshot.

Then we'd head for the state mental hospital through the viaduct, one of those long, deep, concrete drainage washes that run throughout the Los Angeles basin. We used it at night as our tunnel to adventure. We'd scramble down into the dry wash behind the cemetery (there is never water unless it's the rainy season) and walk-run about a mile until we reached what was then known as Spadra State Hospital. It's called Lanterman Developmental Center now, but in those days we just called it Spadra. It was a home for the mentally retarded—maybe that's why I enjoyed myself so much there.

There were usually 10 or 12 of us and we would climb quietly up the side of the wash, up a bridge, and then inside the hospital grounds. On Halloween night, we literally invaded the place, running around the grounds and peeking into windows. One of my friends, Phil Guy—he's now a Commander in the U.S. Navy, I think—pulled himself up to a window to peek in. Unfortunately, one of the residents was peeking out at the same time. They were face to face for about five seconds before Phil screamed and fell into the bushes. Alarms started going off. People were chasing us in jeeps with lights on the tops, and our guys were diving through hedges, running in every direction, and rolling back down into the concrete wash.

We all met up about three hours later back at Bob's Big Boy (our command center) in West Covina, laughing about our escapades and comparing scrapes and bruises.

We had our own rules. If you got caught, you were on your own. None of that all-for-one, one-for-all stuff in our group. We were the best of pals, but we knew we had to take care of ourselves. We'd meet on Sundays to play tackle football without pads. If you got hurt, you got hurt. More than a few guys ended up with broken hands or noses, but that was part of being in our group.

I don't remember getting into any *real* trouble. Oh, maybe once in a while we'd take a joy ride in a car that didn't belong to us—but we figured that was just part of growing up in L.A. Mostly, we channeled our energies into sports, and my senior year we won championships in basketball, football, and baseball. But we always saved enough strength for an occasional light bulb fight.

You've never been in a light bulb fight? We'd go to neighborhood grade schools, form teams, unscrew the light bulbs, and run along the rooftops, jumping from building to building, throwing missiles at each other. Direct hits were great. You'd hear a "pop" and that stuff would be flying all over the place. Unfortunately, one of our marauders, John Eastman, got caught one day and had to pay for all the broken light bulbs. His father was the superintendent of schools.

We tried to limit our breaking and entering but occasionally, after sports practice, we'd raid the school snack bar. Somebody would jimmy the window and two of us would pop into the snack area and throw out all the food. Then we'd sit in the locker room and eat it. The coaches never figured out where we got all the junk food, and I can't imagine how the people running the snack bar ever balanced the books.

All in all, though, we were pretty tame teens—crewcuts, Pendleton shirts, white socks, loafers, cars, hangin' out in the sunshine, listening to music, playing sports, and looking at girls. What else was there? None of us ever had any money. We'd go to Bob's Big Boy, order two cups of coffee and a doughnut. Coffee was 10 cents and so was the doughnut, so for 30 cents—that was 15 cents apiece—two of us could sit at the counter, split the doughnut, drink coffee, and watch the girls. Life in the early sixties sure was simple. Or was it just that I was 17?

Somebody sent me a 25-year history brochure of my high school recently and I was happy to see that tradition was still intact. Our high school was new when I was a freshman (in 1960), and my class of '63 was the first senior class to graduate. We had a lot to do with getting things started. Our senior class built the Quad, a parklike area, with benches and privacy, right in the middle of the school. We got the materials, provided the labor, erected the walls, and planted the grass.

Only seniors were allowed to sit in the Quad. No

one else could even walk through. It was tradition. A senior could go there and have lunch, or talk with his girlfriend, and know that this was his place. We guarded it well, and you'll understand later why our rallying cry was "Over My Dead Body!"

Nevertheless, there was a junior raid. Make that an aborted junior raid. We were tipped by one of the juniors on the football team that others in his class were planning a Saturday night foray to knock down one of the Quad walls. We figured this was a blow against tradition, so we went to war. Our senior group got together that Saturday night—the Dirty Dozen plus others we could trust—and formed committees. We positioned guards with real walkie-talkies, wore dark clothes, blacked our faces, and put on masks. You'd have thought we were commandos. Then we posted lookouts on the rooftops of the campus walkways, sent everyone else back to our central command post, and waited.

We had bags and ropes and guys lying all over the roofs. Then, sure enough, here came the juniors in a procession of cars on the north side of the school. We sent scouts out, and they came back with the news: four carloads and one truck, lights off, full of juniors, and moving slowly.

They never had a chance. As they pulled up behind the school and started to get out, we dropped from the roof, pounding on the cars and screaming like wild men. The juniors driving the cars saw our black faces and ropes, and they stepped on the gas, leaving the others to run. We caught two, tied them up and left them in the parking lot all night. Somebody called the police, probably their parents, and they were untied the following morning.

And I'm told that today, the tradition of the Quad at

Edgewood High remains the same. Seniors only, please. The rest of you have to walk around.

I won my share of sports awards in high school—more than my share, I suppose—but I almost won another kind of award that would have mortified my father, John William, Sr., who had been an excellent athlete himself.

I came within one vote of being named "Best Actor" in school.

Many of the senior athletes were in drama because the teacher, Mrs. Marion Peterson, was a big sports fan and always gave us good grades. The principal never understood why we all wanted Mrs. Peterson's drama class. Actually, it was more than just grades. Mrs. Peterson made drama fun. She formed a group called the Little Oscars Club and they voted on the best actor and actress. Mrs. Peterson said later that she'd never seen a father (mine) more thankful that his son (me) lost by one vote.

In one play, Mrs. Peterson persuaded another football player, Dave Kimball, and me to play old ladies in wigs. We liked it because we got to give grandmotherly hugs to all of the girls in the cast, but it sure was tough finding size 10½ flats to wear with our costumes.

My favorite role, though, was in our senior play, "Over My Dead Body."

I played the body.

No lines.

I just lay there on the floor.

Before the play opened, we borrowed a casket from a local mortuary for publicity pictures, but Mrs. Peterson didn't keep it around very long. I kept popping out of it at odd times.

On opening night I was there in my starring role, no lines, on the floor. The dead body.

But I blew it. I couldn't keep from laughing and everytime I giggled, somebody would walk past and kick me. Now that I think about it, that's probably why I lost the Best Actor award by one vote. Who can vote for a dead body if he can't stay dead?

I looked on it, however, as a learning experience. Anyone who can play a dead body can play for Jim Frey.

I guess we had about a dozen guys in our pack. Most of them went to college and, looking back, I wonder if our midnight military maneuvers didn't influence some of my buddies. Rich Reitan, for example, went into the Air Force Academy while Guy and Davie Kimball went to Annapolis. So with the Navy and Air Force covered, that left the U.S. Marine Corps for me. Off I went for six months of reserve training on the buddy system with my buddy Jim Picano, then 23 years of professional baseball and maneuvers against managers.

First, some background: I had already played 174 minor league baseball games when I joined the U.S. Marine Corps Reserve and was sent to Platoon 291, Camp Pendleton, California, for 16 weeks of basic training.

It was one of those "I've got to do something" situations that confronted every healthy, 18-year-old man in the mid-1960s. My alternatives: remain a ballplaying civilian; get drafted and go to Vietnam; or strangle my minor league manager, Chuck Tanner, and go to prison.

I chose the Marines. Tanner was so strong in those days he probably would have snapped both my wrists. He had sent me down (El Paso to San Jose) during the 1965 season, though, and I figured six months with the Marines would be better than worrying all winter whether or not I would make it in baseball.

So off I went in October 1965 to Camp Pendleton to learn how to execute a three-minute bowel movement. I'm not kidding. I learned other things, too, but crapping in 180 seconds was the hardest.

Almost everything we did during basic training, you see, was at double-time—march to the mess hall, eat standing at attention (always eat the mushy stuff first, I learned, and save the meat to eat on the run), then march to the latrine.

Platoon 291 would be lined up at the latrine, digestive tracks working overtime, each man waiting his turn. Picture the scene: 10 stalls on each side, no doors, no privacy. That's 20 johns for 80 guys and each guy was allotted three minutes, with the other guys standing there, waiting and watching.

I couldn't do it. Not with the next guy standing over me saying, "Hurry up, fer Christsakes!" It was embarrassing. So, for two weeks, I slipped out of the barracks at night, when we were supposed to be sleeping, for my private visit to the latrine.

Then I learned to do it in three minutes. Boy, was I proud!

Actually, I was a model Marine, downright super numerary. My rifle was always clean, uniform was always starched, and the shoes were always shined. I guess that's how I became so neat—sort of the Felix Unger of baseball roommates. Blame it on the Marines.

Being athletic made things easier for me. I was often chosen to lead the platoon in physical training exercises. Some of my buddies had a tougher time. We had guys who couldn't walk without tripping. We had guys who froze with flamethrowers in their hands, and others who couldn't pull the pin on a grenade.

We also had a guy who tried to shoot himself and missed.

Being a bad shot was how he got into such a state in the first place. Every day we'd go to the rifle range, and every day he'd miss. He simply could not qualify. And, every day, he'd get punished for being a bad shot. They'd put him in a manure pit and make him do exercises—push-ups and sit-ups, mostly—while the rest of us marched off for other training.

We all rooted for him because if one man from a platoon couldn't qualify on the rifle range, it reflected on the entire platoon, and we wanted to be number one. But while we were gung ho, he was down in the dung hole, probably wondering if there wasn't a more productive way he could serve his country.

Finally, after five consecutive days of missing targets and doing push-ups in manure, this Marine cracked. He went back to the barracks and tried to shoot himself in the foot with his rifle. I guess he figured a bullet hole in the foot would be a small price to pay for escape from the Marine Corps.

As he pulled the trigger, however, he turned his head away and, sure enough, the bullet went between his toes, barely burning the skin, and ricocheted into the ceiling.

Well, all hell broke loose. Our platoon leaders were so mad they sat the guy on the steps, ordered all of us out of bed and ordered us to march over him, each Marine forced to step on him once as we passed. Then we all had to march up and down the hill outside in full field gear for three hours. But none of us carried live ammunition. It's a good thing. We might not have missed.

My favorite part of being a Marine was the war games. I knew there were far deadlier "games" being played in Vietnam and, frankly, that realization made me attack our exercises with concentration. And, in all honesty, I was fascinated and challenged by military maneuvers.

That's probably how I learned to plan baseball clubhouse jokes so well. I learned that you can't just stumble into an objective. You plan and maneuver— then strike! If Tom Lasorda had known what I was learning in the Marines, he'd have petitioned the President to get me discharged.

We had a major who knew a little about incentives. If we captured his flag during military exercises, we got beer on Saturday nights. Our company always found a way to capture him and it drove him nuts, although I suspect he was secretly proud of us for our ingenuity.

Once he loaded us into helicopters for an overnight exercise in the hills, with nothing to eat or drink except C rations and water (some of the guys tried to smuggle booze into their backpacks but the MPs caught them). The major was positive we were going to have it tough. Choppers ferried us into the middle of nowhere—right to the top of a California mountain, where we made camp. Looking below, however, I spotted a construction camp and climbed down to investigate.

The camp was empty but there was a telephone. Contact!

I telephoned the Pantry Market in Santa Ana and made a deal with the manager, who I knew. He loaded his VW bus with provisions—wine, beer, bread, ham, potato chips, ice, crackers, cookies, and $200 worth of other goodies—and, following the directions I gave him over the phone, he somehow found his way up the construction road on the back side of the mountain. Then we formed committees: some of the company made the 45-minute trek down the back of the mountain to bring up the food; the others dug a six-foot-deep pit for the ice. We brought everything up, then camouflaged the wine, beer, and food by covering it with a poncho, leaves, and brush.

It was a great night for the 20 guys in our company. Other guys in the distance were eating cold C rations while we sat around a fire roasting hot dogs and marshmallows, sipping wine out of our canteens, and singing at the top of our lungs.

Then the major showed up. He couldn't believe what he was hearing when somebody offered him a hot dog. Somebody else gave him a cigar, and somebody asked if he'd like a cold beer.

"I give up," he said. "I'm impressed. Just don't tell me how you did it." Then he joined the party.

It was not always a party for our young Marines. I'll never forget our first Camp Pendleton inspection, scheduled one Saturday at noon. If we passed, we would receive our first overnight passes since the beginning of basic training. Everybody was primed for Saturday night in nearby Oceanside. Some were even ready to hitch rides back home to Los Angeles.

The inspecting sergeant, however, was unhappy with our broom closet.

"It's dirty," he said. "Clean it. I'll be back in two hours."

Two hours later he returned, didn't like the way the latrine looked, and said:

"Clean it. I'll be back at 5 o'clock."

By now we were getting impatient (after all, the girls somewhere were waiting.) So we attacked the latrine with 80 guys and made it spotless.

But at 5 o'clock the sergeant didn't like the way his quarter bounced off one of the beds. He ripped it apart and told us he'd be back in three hours.

This time he showed up with a gunnery sergeant and staff sergeant wearing white gloves, who opened one guy's foot-locker, found the contents out of order, dumped it onto the floor, and walked out.

"We'll be back at 10 o'clock," said the sergeant.

Now there was panic. We remade every bed and reorganized every foot locker. We were ready.

At 10 o'clock, though, the creep with the white gloves ran his finger behind the venetian blinds and came out with dirt.

"See you at midnight," he said.

It was our last gasp. We formed details of five men each to inspect what everyone else had cleaned. Then we had another guy inspect what the inspection details had inspected. We were perfect and we knew it. It would be late, but there was no way we weren't getting out of there.

Exactly at midnight, they showed up—our sergeant, the gunny, the staff, the corporal, and a first lieutenant. Slowly, they walked the entire barracks, asking questions, looking at everything.

"I'm impressed," said the lieutenant. "But why am I here at midnight?"

Then he turned to the sergeant and said: "These men need to be taught a lesson."

At that, the corporal took a bucket of sand, threw it across the barracks, and yelled, "Clean it again!"

We got the point. They hadn't planned to give us overnight passes in the first place.

And my baseball roomies wondered how I became so neat.

There was a time when I was sure I would also go to Vietnam, even though I had only enlisted for the reserve program. During my active duty, the war escalated from 220,000 troops in Vietnam to more than 500,000 and all of us began to wonder if we would be next. Luckily, my number didn't come up. The escalation slowed and I finished my reserve training in a communications group attached to the U.S. Navy at Los Alamitos. A lot of the guys from my earlier platoon went into the Military Police and landed in Saigon just a few days before the Tet offensive. I was told later than more than 50 percent of them didn't return.

The Marines cut me no slack because I was a professional ballplayer. Most of my superiors didn't know or care. Several even tried to persuade me to reenlist by promising promotions. I was only 19 when I left the Marines in March 1966, later to serve two-week hitches during the off-seasons until my reserve obligation was complete, and I didn't even know if I would play more baseball.

For one thing, I had refused to return to El Paso, where Tanner was manager. I was convinced he didn't like me and I knew I didn't like him, but I was a cocky kid then, so what did I know? People from the Angels, who owned my contract, tried to persuade me but I wouldn't budge. Then my mother told me to go back to El Paso, and I went. Good Marines don't argue with their mothers.

So in April 1966 I was back in El Paso, Texas (Double-A), without benefit of spring training but, because of the Marines, in better physical condition than anyone else on the team.

Then came the breaks. Ten days after going to El Paso, two players from the Angels' Triple-A club in Seattle, Mike White and Al Spangler, went down. White dislocated his shoulder while diving for a ball and Spangler had four wisdom teeth pulled on the same day. Seattle needed help, I was hitting .360 after seven games, and I got the call.

Ten weeks later Rick Reichardt of the Angels needed a kidney operation and, once again, the phone rang for help. Who did Seattle have who was ready for the big leagues? Well, nobody actually, but this kid Johnstone is hitting .340 so how about him?

It happened that quickly. I went from learning how to take a crap in three minutes and smuggling wine to a mountaintop to playing major league baseball, all in less than a year.

Now, more than 20 years later with my baseball career ended and a different life ahead, I think back about those days with the U.S. Marines.

And I wonder whatever happened to the guy who couldn't cut it, tried to shoot himself, and missed.

I wonder also about the guys from my outfit who did cut it, only to lose their lives in Vietnam.

There was a winter night about a year ago in Washington, D.C.—actually it was about 2:30 A.M., following an appearance I made on Larry King's nationally syndicated radio show—when I decided to visit the Vietnam Memorial.

It was something I felt I had to do, and the middle of the night seemed like a good time. So I took flowers with me to the radio studio, then walked outside after the show, flagged a taxi, and told the driver my destination.

"You figure I'm a little strange, huh?" I said to the driver.

"Not really," he said. "You'd be surprised how many guys I've brought out here alone after everybody else has gone home."

So I paid my visit while the taxi driver waited. If you haven't visited the Vietnam Memorial, located across from the Lincoln Memorial, I wish you would if you get the chance. It's beautiful, especially at night, and there is no way you can walk along that wall and look at those 55,000 names—listed by the years in which they died while serving their country—without feeling the deep impact of what happened in Vietnam.

I placed the flowers and looked on the wall for names I might recognize. There were some. There were others I wasn't sure about. It didn't matter. On that lonely, cold morning in Washington, D.C., I felt like I knew all of them, and I said a prayer, thanking them for what they did for me and my country.

"

Lasorda suggested that perhaps the umpire was (a) gutless or (b) blind. The umpire then suggested that Lasorda (a) leave the premises and (b) immediately. That's when baseball's Goodwill Ambassador began to undress on the mound.

4
BUT IT'S BETTER THAN PITTSBURGH

Mary Jayne, my wife, was headed out the door one day last winter when I said, "Hey, remember all the fun we had when I played winter ball down in Puerto Rico?"

She stopped dead still, made a full turn to look me in the eye, and I knew I'd made a mistake.

"Fun? Did you say fun?

"Do you mean like stuffing tinfoil into the vents at night so the rats wouldn't get into the apartment? Saving rat rags to jam under the door? Going to a swimming pool full of algae in the mornings and filling buckets so we would have water to flush the toilets?

"You said fun? Like that crazy wife of your teammate who would sunbathe on a two-foot ledge outside her eighth-floor apartment that had no railing? And wasn't that the apartment where the mainte-

43

nance man got mad at the owner who lived on the 10th floor so he cut the elevator cable and two people fell eight floors?

"Fun? Yes, darling," she continued, "I really had fun that day the door jammed. One of the wives had two babies locked inside the apartment and had to race downtown on a motor scooter to get the fire department to break down the door.

"And how about that wonderful little revolution? One day the kid was boxing our groceries at the market, the next day he was standing on our corner in uniform, carrying a rifle. That was exciting— especially when they blew up the waterworks and the toilets wouldn't flush.

"Winter ball was disgusting, that's what it was! We were living in a sleaze box. My kitchen was dark brown, the size of a closet, and the only reason we had a Christmas tree was because I stood in line all night to get one of the scraggly, little trees that Sears was selling. Don't you remember? That's why they had the party at our place. We had the only tree.

"But you just wanted the fun stories, right? How about taking the inter-island airlines when you'd buy a ticket and wait for the loudspeaker to tell you at which gate the next plane would be landing. One hundred people would race to the gate to fight for 14 seats. Don't you remember how we missed the first two planes before you dragged me by the arm and my heels broke and I was screaming?

"I liked it, too, when the pilot—who was also the steward and mechanic—came back to pull down all the window shades so the Americans wouldn't see how low we were flying over the mountains so he could save gas.

"And remember how romantic it was when we'd go

with another couple to the drive-in movie? First we'd buy an orange and peel it. Then we'd take the seats out of the jeep and put them on the ground. Two people would sit on the ground and the lucky ones got to sit on the hood of the jeep.

"God, that was fun. I remember laying linoleum on a sand floor. I remember serving lima beans and hamburger for three months because there was a dock strike and we couldn't get any other meat except for that scraggly chicken one of the players stole from somebody's front yard. I also remember going to a bookstore one day and getting trapped for two hours because a rat as big as a possum wouldn't get out of the hallway to the front door.

"And how about the player who wanted to earn some extra money? Where did he get all of that bamboo he made those bongs out of? From the side of the road, wasn't it, and he sold the bongs to locals for $50. Then there was the wife of one of the black players who tried to throw the wife of one of the white players off the balcony. I thought that was a little scary.

"But you know, Jay, you're right. That really was fun. What made you ask, honey, are you thinking about making a comeback?"

Sometimes Mary Jayne really bugs me. I thought winter ball was fun, but in retrospect, Puerto Rico probably did look better from center field than it did from a crumbling apartment or crowded bus. Nevertheless, I spent three enjoyable years playing for teams from Ponce and Caguas, P.R., during the 1960s and early 1970s and Mary Jayne-with-the-good-memory was right about one thing: it was no vacation.

Those folks took their baseball seriously and still do.

We *Americanos* who went south during the winters did so for a couple of reasons: money and playing time. Clubs would send youngsters into Central and South America with instructions to work on parts of their game.

It still works that way in the eighties, except in a somewhat different context. They still take their pennant races seriously in the Dominican Republic, Puerto Rico, Venezuela, and Mexico, but you don't see as many American youngsters there as before. Instead, you find more experienced Triple-A players than in the past.

Why the shift? Because of the expansion of instructional leagues in Arizona and Florida. Major league teams prefer nowadays to keep their young draft choice signees within the boundaries of the United States and under more direct control of competent instructors.

The need for money has also changed. Twenty years ago a Steve Sax might hit .332 for the Dodgers and still go south to pick up additional pocket money. Nowadays he can stay home and earn more smiling into a TV camera or endorsing a product. Major league salaries, too, have escalated far beyond what a player can earn in Puerto Rico.

And, there are the horror stories about winter ball. Long and dangerous bus rides, scary food and living conditions, local ownership backing out on contracts, and other nightmares. An awful lot of guys have gone south and come back grumbling. Let's face it—everybody doesn't have the survival qualities of Tom Lasorda.

Let me give you an example: He was managing the

Escogido club in the Dominican League and had taken his team to Santiago, about 100 miles from the capital of Santo Domingo, his club's hometown. Lasorda's team was leading, 3–1, in the bottom of the ninth and Doyle Alexander was pitching against a guy named Tom Silverio, a native of Santiago who later played a few seasons with the Angels in the early 1970s. Silverio hit a long ball over rightfielder Von Joshua's head, but Von played the bounce perfectly off the wall and threw the runner out at third base.

But no. The umpire, a Dominican named Elias Frias, was signaling "home run" and Lasorda went berserk as only Lasorda can do.

"How can you call that a home run?" he screamed.

"The ball went out of the park," said the umpire.

"Out of the park? Then how did my rightfielder get the ball to throw out the runner at third base?"

"He took it out of his pocket," said Frias.

The disbelieving Lasorda ran to home plate umpire George Blanford, an American, and said "Did you see a home run?"

"I don't know," said Blanford. "I didn't see anything."

Lasorda then suggested that perhaps Blanford was (a) gutless or (b) blind. Blanford then suggested that Lasorda (a) leave the premises and (b) immediately.

That's when baseball's Goodwill Ambassador began to undress. In the middle of the diamond.

He threw his cap into the stands. He took off one shoe and fired it over third. He took off the other and sailed it into the stands behind first base. Then he ripped off his shirt, revealing that beautiful bare chest, threw the shirt into the air, and stomped off the field.

End of show, right? Alexander retired the next

hitter, Lasorda's team won, 3–2, and Lasorda went singing into the shower.

Except that when he came out of the shower, soldiers with rifles were in his locker room.

"Get your clothes on," said the guy wearing the most ribbons. "You're coming with us."

Now Tito Fuentes, Matty Alou, and other Escogido players tried to intervene, but the soldiers were adamant.

"He's going to jail," said the guy with the ribbons. But Lasorda figured it was a joke, so off he went.

They locked him up. And he spent all night in that Santiago jail. "I stood up all night," he told me later. "The only way to pass the time was to pretend I was in church at mass. I went over every part of the mass."

He was released the following morning and the explanation was that one of the army generals had attended the game and had wagered on Santiago. And when Lasorda had gone over the edge, the general had turned to another officer and said, "Look at that! Why don't our managers argue like that for our team? Go lock him up for indecent exposure, anyhow!"

"You mean to tell me," said Lasorda, after hearing the explanation, "that if a general in the stands doesn't like what happens on the field he can lock me up?"

"That's the tough part of baseball in Santiago," Lasorda was told.

So what did Lasorda do about it? He called a press conference, but instead of being indignant or threatening anybody, he stood in front of the Dominican press and said how much he enjoyed spending the night in jail. He mentioned how friendly the other six prisoners had been and praised the hospitality of his jailers.

Then everybody laughed and went home.

Winter ball, however, isn't always laughs and you can't always go home.

Ed Herrmann, for example, is one of the funniest guys I ever knew. He played with five different major league teams during 11 seasons (most of my pals are well-traveled) and caught 817 major league games.

That's why he has no feeling in his hands these days. He's now a mechanic for Mercedes and he's having trouble feeling the torque wrench. That's what happens when you catch too many baseballs on your fingertips. Calcium builds up, circulation goes, and you can't feel the torque wrench anymore.

Anyhow, Hermy is playing one winter with Bill Melton in Venezuela and there are no laughs, period. Melton is hitting .180, Herrmann about .190, and both of them are trying like crazy to get out of there and back home. Hermy is even hurt. His hand is swollen and hurting like hell, but they won't release him. He goes to a doctor, but the ballclub is owned by doctors and the x-rays come back negative. They tell him his hand is not fractured and that he should be playing to earn his pay.

Well, Hermy sends off the x-rays to the Chicago White Sox's doctor, who finds a crack and tells Hermy he should come home. Still no deal. The Venezuelan doctors say there is no crack and that Hermy should play. Hermy is going nuts.

So one night Melton comes home to his apartment, right next door to Herrmann, and he hears this thumping through the wall. All night long he hears this thumping. Eddie is banging his hand against the head of the bed. He wants to crack it.

The next day Eddie walks into the front office, shows his hand—which by then resembles a piece of stuffed salami—and says, "Are you satisfied? That son of a bitch is broken and I want to go home!"

It worked. Hermy went home. But at last report he was thinking about surgery so he could feel the torque wrench again.

That was the winter of 1970, the same year that South Americans discovered that Bill Melton was not Babe Ruth. Actually, my pal from Gulfport, Mississippi, now a successful businessman in Orange County, looks a little like the Bambino but maybe a little prettier. And, on occasion, Melton had the same kind of power. Melton hit 160 home runs during a 10-year big league career, including back-to-back years of 33 each with the White Sox in 1970 and 1971.

That's what was so crazy about his winter of '70. Bill had just hit 23 dingers during the 1969 season in Chicago and, at age 24, was poised to become the home-run king of the major leagues.

But that wasn't enough for Luis Aparicio, who had signed Melton, Herrmann, and Walt "No-Neck" Williams to play for his Maracaibo team. Little Louie told everybody in Venezuela that Melton was the next Babe Ruth, and for a salary of $3,000 a month that's what they expected. A throng showed up the first day of practice just to see the big gringo take batting practice.

What happened after that was so awful it was hilarious. Melton, to paraphrase the learned Ambassador Lasorda, suddenly couldn't hit water from a boat with a paddle. He homered in the bottom of the ninth in front of 35,000 fanatics the first night in town and didn't hit another home run for 50 games. They damn near lynched him.

He ended up with one HR and four RBI, and had to get the Secretary of State to sign his visa before he could leave Maracaibo. He also had to write a letter apologizing to the city for being such a stiff.

The Maracaibo team even tried trading Melton for Graig Nettles but that didn't work, either. Finally, they just accepted his letter of apology and sent him off to Chicago, where he hit 33 home runs with 96 RBI the next season. You figure it out.

"I did one good deed while I was there," Melton told me later. "I saved Nettles's life."

Melton and Nettles had gone to a racetrack in Venezuela, paying $1.50 to share a taxi. On the way back to their hotel, however, a different taxi driver tried to charge them $20 and Nettles refused to pay.

"He's right there in the cab driver's face yelling at him," said Melton, "and I look down into the seat and see this guy holding a gun. All of a sudden $20 didn't seem like so much to me."

Melton never did have much luck with winter ball. He went to Puerto Rico to play for a man named Gonzalez and Bill's first request was for a telephone in his apartment.

"I don't know," said Gonzalez. "It's going to cost a lot of money."

"But I need a telephone," said Melton. He then walked into the cage and hit about five or six balls out of the park during batting practice.

"OK, OK" said Gonzalez, "you get a telephone."

But after the first week of the season—after going 0 for 35 at the plate—Melton returned home after a game to discover his telephone was gone.

"You no hit, you no talk," said Gonzalez.

Trivia question: Who was the last American winter league batting champion of Nicaragua?

My jeweler, Richard Alan Scheinblum of Fort Apache–The Bronx, New York, was the last Nicaraguan batting champ. He edged Doug Rader to lead the league in 1966 with a .337 batting average and it almost killed him.

Richie was playing outfield for Cinco Estrellas in the seventh game of the Nicaraguan playoffs and it just so happens that *Cinco Estrellas* means "Five Stars" and was named after the general who backed the team, military dictator Anastasio Somoza Debayle. Opposing Somoza's team that day was La Boer, the team representing the unhappy folks who were about to start a revolution.

"Because I played for Cinco Estrellas, the people automatically assumed I was with the military," recalls Scheinblum. "I'd walk around all day saying 'no politco . . . no politico,' but it wasn't doing much good. I was a marked man.

"So we're in the seventh game and although we don't know it, the revolution is scheduled to begin when the game ended. I had just hit a three-run homer in the eighth inning to put us ahead, too. Nice timing.

"Well, the game ends and we win, and all hell breaks loose. Everybody from the stands runs into the outfield and who are they after? Me! Next thing I know I'm on the ground getting kicked and beaten. I thought I was a dead man, but two of my teammates—a left-handed pitcher named Jim Weaver and my roomie, Steve Boros—somehow dragged me away from the crowd back into our dugout tunnel.

"By the time we got away from the park that night you could hear gunfire all over the city. We spent the night doing push-ups under our beds in the hotel. The windows had already been shot out, I'm a nervous wreck, and there's Boros in the corner taking notes for a book he wants to write.

"By morning the revolution was going full blast. The only reason we got out of the country was because the revolutionaries were holding 28 American hostages at the Grand Hotel and we used their air reservations. Hey, all is fair. Nobody really knew what was going on but we knew it was serious. One of our guys had a radio and we heard that one person had been reported wounded. One person? There were nine people lying dead in our street! Man, it was just like a scene out of *The Year of Living Dangerously*. We were running barricades in taxis to the airfield and people were shooting at us.

"But we made it and there hasn't really been any organized winter baseball there since. I guess having a Jewish kid from the Bronx win the batting title was just too much for them."

Richie, who spent eight years in the majors with seven different teams (what did I tell you about my friends?), also had the distinct pleasure of playing in Venezuela in 1968, where he experienced one of the most embarrassing events ever recorded in baseball history.

"I was dehydrated because of my diet," said Richie. "I was losing weight and hadn't had a bowel movement in three weeks. We drive all night from Caracas over this incredibly dangerous mountain road—everybody knows it, 365 curves taking you to the edge of death, one for each day of the year—and we reached our destination, a whorehouse in Maracaibo, at 10 A.M.. As we arrived, the girls were leaving. That was the deal. When the visiting baseball team came to town, it was billeted at this bordello. When we were finished, the girls returned. I guess they figured they were getting maximum efficiency that way.

"Anyhow, we had about an hour to change clothes after our terrifying trip and we were at the ballpark by 11 A.M. And I'm not kidding when I say it was 138 degrees and humid.

"In my first at-bat, I slap a blooper into the outfield, round first at full speed, and slide into second.

"And as I slid, I emptied into my pants. God, did I smell awful. I look up from the ground into the eyes of the shortstop, Luis Aparicio, and he says, 'Are you OK?'

" 'No problem,' I answered, 'I've got elastic on the bottom of my pants.'

"They had to send a stretcher to carry me off the field, with each guy holding the stretcher with one hand and his nose with the other.

"You know how some guys carry batting gloves in their back pockets? For the rest of that season I carried toilet paper."

Orlando Cepeda, the Baby Bull from Ponce, Puerto Rico, has his own believe-it-or-not tale from winter baseball.

It was one of those Caribbean World Series experiences—Puerto Rico playing at Nicaragua, with Cepeda and the Puerto Ricans leading 5–0. All of a sudden, Nicaraguan players called timeout and came across the field.

"We're winning," they said.

"What do you mean you're winning?" said the Puerto Ricans.

"We're winning."

"No, you're not winning."

"We're winning," the Nicaraguans insisted.

Just about then, soldiers in the stands started firing machine guns into the air.

"You know what?" Cepeda said to the Nicaraguan manager, "Not only are you winning—you win."

The locals usually won, too, against *Americanos* who ventured south to play baseball.

Like the time in Caguas, P.R., 1974, when Jim Essian and I were playing chess and minding our own business in the back seat of an automobile being driven by Bobby Wine. We were out there in the middle of nowhere, headed for Mayaguez, when a red station wagon driven by a local lady pulled suddenly onto the highway in front of us.

Bobby swerved, but there was no avoiding the crash. Chess pieces—not to mention a few auto parts—flew everywhere, but, luckily, nobody was hurt. There was damage, however, and Bobby ended up in front of a Puerto Rican judge.

Actually, he had to wait for the judge to finish his game of dominoes before he would hear the case. Wine was instructed by an interpreter not to talk, even though he had been driving. The interpreter did all the talking, and talking, and talking. Then the judge did a lot of talking, none of which Bobby understood.

"Now what?" asked Bobby finally.

"Now we go to trial," said the interpreter.

"But what did we just do?"

"The judge was scolding the woman because he said it was her fault."

So Wine gets a lawyer through the ballclub and goes to court. This time he hears everybody talking back and forth until, finally, the interpreter tells him to plead guilty.

"What?"

"Plead guilty," said the interpreter, "and it only costs you $5 and the whole thing is settled. We can leave."

So Bobby pleaded guilty, paid the $5, and forgot about it.

Except that three months later the lady came back with some high-powered legal counsel and sued him for $300,000. After all, she had the court transcript right there—the American was guilty and had admitted it!

I never did find find how much Bobby and the ballclub had to pay to settle that case. I'm still trying to replace the chess pieces that went flying out the window.

One of the other problems Wine faced as a manager in the Caribbean was the same problem managers face in the big leagues: the owners.

A lot of people are promised jobs, you see, and it often happens that a manager in winter ball finds himself with a 25-man roster and another 10 guys hanging around waiting for the job they were promised. Then along comes an owner who wants to make trades or activate new players, just so that he can keep all the people he promised to hire happy.

A Puerto Rican owner walked into Wine's office one day and said, "We've got to make a trade."

"Why?" asked Wine. "We're in first place by eight games, we've got a good team, and everybody's contributing. Why trade?"

"Because the fans don't think we're trying," said the owner. "We've got to do something."

So the man traded one of Bobby's pitchers for a young, backup catcher who wasn't good enough to play. About three days after the deal was made, the owner walked back into Wine's office and said, "We have to get a pitcher."

That's winter ball.

So is risking your life every time your team goes on the road. I've been on some insane, curvy, mountain roads in Puerto Rico. How curvy? You could see the back end of the bus from the front end, that's how curvy. No guard rails on the roads, either, and when a tractor trailer comes honking down the mountain from the other direction, things get tight.

One time, so help me, I saw our bus driver crossing himself as he started to take us over the mountain.

That's winter ball.

Mike Schmidt, Essian, and I shared an apartment one winter in Puerto Rico (Mary Jayne had seen enough), but we hardly knew Essian was around. He was into transcendental meditation in those days and did a lot of sitting around, mumbling phrases to himself. Mike and I just stared at him and mumbled phrases of our own, but I don't think he ever heard us.

The guy who provided us with a car heard us, though, because every week the car broke down. There was an agency, you see, that had a deal with the Caguas ballclub. This particular guy took great pride in providing cars for ballplayers.

But we drove him nuts. First the tires went bad, so we returned the car and got a different one. Then the carburetor conked out and we exchanged that car, too. And it always seemed to happen just as the car needed a tank of gas. So we'd take it back and get another car with a full tank.

It got so the guy would stand out front waiting for us. For nine weeks in a row something was always breaking or falling off the car he gave us.

When we were down to our final two weeks in Puerto Rico, this car dealer outdid himself. He gave us a beauty: a mustard-yellow Ford, brand new top to bottom.

"You will be happy with this," he said. "I stake my job on this car. It will not give you trouble."

And it didn't. That car gave us no trouble as long as we had it. Four days after we got it I came home with groceries and parked the Ford. Schmidt wanted to use the car, but 15 minutes after going downstairs, he came back.

"Where *is* the car?" asked Schmidt.

"Right next to the elevator," I said.

"No it isn't."

"Yes it is. How can you miss it?"

"There is no car down there," said Schmidt, and he was right.

It had been stolen.

Have you ever heard of a runner on second base getting thrown out sliding *back into second base* on a base hit into left field?

It happened to Professor Backwards in the Dominican Republic.

The Professor is Joe Ferguson in real life, the former major league catcher who now coaches under manager Bobby Valentine for the Texas Rangers. Fergy and Bobby both played under Lasorda in the Dominican, where Professor Backwards gained immortality.

The situation: Tom Paciorek was the hitter, one out, with Fergy the runner at second base after doubling. Lasorda was managing and also coaching third base. His team had lost seven in a row, so you can imagine his mood.

Paciorek singled, a grounder between third and shortstop, but unquestionably a hit into left field. Now, the quiz: Will Ferguson (a) score from second, (b) get thrown out at home plate, (c) get thrown out at third base, or (d) remain on second base?

None of the above.

The Professor, you see, had been dancing off second when Paciorek hit the ball and, as the shortstop made a futile lunge, Fergy hesitated. Then he sees the ball headed into left field but figures with his late start that he might get thrown out. Ahhh, but Fergy is no dummy. He says to himself, "I'll trick the left fielder and go back to second."

Paciorek, meanwhile, is ecstatic. He hadn't gotten an RBI in a month and he figures this one is a lock. But as he rounds first, what does he see? Lasorda waving for Ferguson to score and Ferguson sliding back into second.

The left fielder, meanwhile, is mystified. He had such a weak arm he couldn't have thrown out Mary Jayne pushing a baby carriage. His arm is so weak, in fact, that he never even considers throwing to third base. All he wants to do is flip the ball back to second base to hold Paciorek to a single.

Imagine his surprise when his flip to the second baseman nails Fergy sliding back.

Lasorda is livid and screaming something about "... never in 27 years of baseball have I seen anything like that ..." as Fergy comes jogging off the field. So what does Joe say?

"Gee, Tommy, I don't know why you're so upset. That play could happen to anyone."

He's been called Professor Backwards ever since.

But this story tops them all. It's not as funny as it is strange, but it does sum up the bizarre world of winter ball, although I can't say that Brant Alyea's story is typical.

Brant Alyea, who spent six seasons as a power-hitting yet part-time outfielder with four major league teams, is now 46 years old and works as a casino floorman at the Tropicana Hotel in Atlantic City, New Jersey, close to his hometown of Passaic.

Brant's 21-year-old son, Brant Alyea, Jr., is property of the Toronto Blue Jays and perhaps only a few years away from becoming a major league star.

Their story goes as far over the edge as you can go.

Let us go back 20 years to Nicaragua, to that incredible championship game between Cinco Estrellas and La Boer, the game that ended as the revolution began, that same game in which Richie Scheinblum escaped with his life, then fled gunfire and Nicaragua with other American ballplayers.

Alyea was one of the players in that ill-fated game, and he left a baby son behind. And what happened during the following decade is so bizarre, so unbelievable, yet so true, that I won't try to relate it. I asked Brant Alyea to do it and these are his words, his story:

"On the night the shooting started I thought I'd be smart, so I put my luggage in the Grand Hotel, only to discover the next day that tanks had surrounded the place and my luggage had been confiscated. I left anyway, with the rest of the guys, bricks hitting our taxi windows, the whole frightening scene. And since

I had no luggage, I was the first person to pass through customs when we hit the United States. The news people zeroed in on me and started asking questions. But I knew better than to say anything political. I could only say 'I'm a ballplayer. There's a lot of turmoil down there. I don't know what's happening.'

"What I didn't tell them was that I had left a son behind. I didn't want anything to happen to him or his mother.

"I had played in Nicaragua one year earlier, you see, in 1965, the same year I was a rookie with the Washington Senators. While there, I dated a Nicaraguan girl, Melania Medina, a nurse in a hospital. We saw a lot of each other but we left it at that. When winter ball was finished I went back to the U.S.

"But when I returned again in 1966, the year all the fighting broke out, I was met at the plane by one of the Nicaraguan players on our team.

" 'Come with me,' he said. 'I want to show you something.' And he took me to the Medina home, where I found Melania holding a baby. She said it was mine and I had no reason to doubt her. The family was very apprehensive, not because we were unmarried, but because they wanted the baby to have my name. So I signed the papers, they held a fiesta, everybody hugged everybody, and nobody said anything about getting married because there would be no shame. Everybody was happy, including Melania, who brought the baby to games all season.

"Then all hell broke loose. Before I left the country I left Melania $1,000 and promised to come back. But I couldn't get back. I kept track of them for a while through the child's godfather, a Cuban ballplayer named Pancho Herrera. He sent me a report once, when the boy was 10, that he had gotten big and was playing baseball in the streets. Melania, meanwhile, got married to a man who lives in Venezuela—they have three daughters now—and she is allowed to come and go between her native country and Venezuela. Only men cannot leave Nicaragua.

"As time went along, I lost track of the boy but never the awareness that he was there. When I'd see the fighting in the streets of Nicaragua on television I'd say to friends 'It feels so strange to know I have a son down there, perhaps one of those kids holding a gun.'

"Then, about a year and a half ago we were standing around the casino one day talking baseball and one of the bosses had a magazine that listed 70 major leaguers who also had sons playing professional ball. And there it was: Brant Alyea, Jr., was hitting .333 for Medicine Hat in a rookie league in Canada.

"It was my kid and he was a pro ballplayer and I didn't even know it! So I rushed to the telephone and contacted him through the Blue Jays. Apparently he had wanted to reach me but didn't speak English. Besides, the Blue Jays had discouraged it. Some bonehead in their front office thought there might be a stigma attached to me working in Atlantic City where there's gambling. Anyway, he hadn't called.

"The following winter I went to Clearwater, Florida, to meet him at Toronto's minor league spring training complex and, yeah, there were some tears. But I want to tell you that this kid is gonna be a player. It turns out that at age 17 he was 6'4", 170, and the best player in Nicaragua. That's why he didn't have to go into the army. He just played ball.

"How he got out of the country is the damnedest

thing. First he went to Canada with the Nicaraguan national team to play in a 10-day tournament against Cuba, Canada, and the U.S. Well, he was voted MVP and that's where the Blue Jays spotted him. They sent Eppy Guerrero, their hotshot scout [coordinator of Latin American scouting and player development] to Nicaragua. Eppy took a real chance, too. He dressed in a Sandinista uniform to gain entrance to the stadium to see Brant play. No telling what would have happened if he'd been caught because there was no way they wanted this kid to leave the country to play ball in America.

"So Eppy offers him a contract—not as much money as some other clubs had mentioned because by now Brant was no longer a secret—but he figured Eppy had the best chance of getting him out of Nicaragua, so Brant signed for a $6,000 bonus and gave the money to his mother.

"Then the Blue Jays had to figure out how to get him out. First they sent $2,000 to his aunt to use for bribe money. Then the aunt went with Brant to the airport, where he told the soldiers at customs that he wanted to fly to Venezuela to visit his mother.

" 'We can't let you go,' he was told, 'because you might not come back.' I guess that's when he flashed the bribe money, but it still didn't do any good. They were afraid to let him go. Then Brant said 'OK' and started to walk away, but one of the customs officials caught him and said, 'Let's take a look at that $2,000.' That's how he got out.

"So last year in Class A ball he hit .280 with 10 home runs and 55 RBI and made the all-star team, even though he got spiked, broke his hand, and missed eight weeks of the season. This year [1987] I'm hoping he'll either play A ball again or move up to

Double-A in Knoxville, Tennessee. I think he's only two years away—I mean, this kid is going to knock fences down. He's 6'5" now and still has a 32-inch waist. I figure he'll eventually weigh 215, since I've had him on a weight program and better diet. He stayed with me for seven weeks in Atlantic City before going back down to Venezuela to play winter ball. He's got great hands and a strong arm. He's agile, too, but he doesn't have that Rickey Henderson speed. Neither did I.

"It turns out that when he was playing ball as a kid down there he took pride in being my son. He was motivated because a lot of people remembered me. I had led the league in home runs both years I was there and he had seen pictures of me.

"It's just that we were never in touch. For all those years, we hadn't spoken to each other. Now he's here with me, when he isn't in Venezuela or playing ball with the Toronto organization, and I think it's fantastic. He still telephones his friends back in Nicaragua but he knows he can't go back, just like I couldn't go back 20 years ago."

Didn't I tell you it was a strange story?

And you'll probably be hearing more about the Alyeas. Some people in Hollywood are talking TV movie and they'd like to get Martin Sheen and his son, Emilio Estevez, to play the roles.

I'm wondering, meanwhile, if I could have fun with Mary Jayne by telling her there is a kid ballplayer down in Puerto Rico named Jay-sus who wears giant sunglasses and a Star Patrol helmet.

She'd probably just say I was bragging again.

At midnight—you could set your watch by it—the doors would fly open and guys would start having contests in the corridor. Hitting golf balls, pillow fights, Whiffle balls, whatever. The belly-bumping competition was the best.

5

BEDCHECK BLUES AND THE FINE ART OF BELLY-BUMPING

Can you imagine the Philly Fanatic or San Diego Chicken goosing Joe DiMaggio? A girl in short shorts supplying baseballs to Jocko Conlan and giving him a kiss at home plate? Ty Cobb trying to field a ball that had just bounded 30 feet into the air after landing behind shortstop?

Yes, there have been some changes in baseball, most of them since I first put on a California Angels uniform as a teenager in 1966. Some have improved the game, some certainly haven't.

The changes have made considerable impact— divisional playoffs into the middle of October, World Series games into the middle of the night, designated hitters, domed stadiums, artificial turf, free agency, multi-year contracts, arbitration, agents, drug testing, contract buyouts, and that ever-popular disabled list.

Also, no more roomies.

When baseball teams did away with roommates on the road, something got lost—camaraderie, team togetherness, whatever you want to call it. But today's players negotiated for single-room privacy and that's what they got.

I've had enough baseball roommates to stock a franchise, maybe an entire organization, and certainly a carnival act, which is where most of them belong.

My idea of an ideal roomie:

Somebody you can talk to, particularly late at night ("Is that son of a bitch ever gonna play me or not?").

Somebody who will answer the phone and alibi for you when your wife calls ("You're not going to believe this, Mary Jayne, but the archbishop invited Jay out for dinner, the moat flooded, the phone lines are out, and nobody can reach him").

Somebody who likes the same TV programs you like ("What channel has pro wrestling?").

Somebody who will cover for you at curfew ("Hey, Rooms, this is me calling in . . . ahh, listen, can you pack my suitcase and meet me at the plane in the morning?").

Somebody who will say sympathetic things when things are going badly ("Don't let the manager bother you. He's an idiot, anyhow.").

Somebody who will pick up the dinner check ("My turn again?").

Somebody who doesn't snore, but doesn't mind if you do.

Albie Pearson and Ted Kluszewski were ideal roomies. Albie stood 5'5" and weighed 140. Klu was 6'2", 240.

But they got along famously. Whenever Albie got frisky, big Klu would simply say, "Shut up, you little runt, or I'll make you sleep in the dresser drawer."

I was the Mr. Clean of roommates—like I said, Felix Unger in spikes. I even vacuumed. If my roomie would come home staggering and throw his trousers into the corner, he'd wake up thinking they were lost somewhere. Later, he'd find them hanging in the closet where they belonged. U.S. Marine J. Johnstone ready for inspection, sir!

Same subject, small digression: After we were first married, I drove Mary Jayne crazy with my neatness. She'd clean all day and I'd come home, see something on the floor, and start the vacuum. It would even make her madder when I couldn't hear her screaming over the noise.

I even won a game for the Phillies once because I was neat. The bases were loaded, yours truly was at bat, the pitcher throws a ball into the dirt and it hits my foot. I started toward first base, but the umpire objected.

"Come back and hit," he said.

"But the ball hit my foot."

"I don't think so."

"I'll prove it. Go look at the ball."

And, sure enough, the ball was smudged with fresh, red shoe polish.

"See, I shine my shoes every night," I told the ump. He awarded me first base and the winning run was forced home from third.

"I'm proud of Johnstone," Phils manager Danny Ozark told sportswriters later. "He's the only guy on this team who shines his shoes at least twice a day."

He didn't stay proud very long, however. He was looking for me the next day and couldn't find me. I was back in the equipment room ironing my uniform shirt.

But back to roomies. Jim Fregosi was one of my favorites.

He'd always cover for me when I'd be out past curfew (usually doing volunteer work at a nearby mission or getting locked in the library after closing hours).

But my favorite curfew story isn't even related to baseball. It concerns Ken Herock, tight end with the Raiders, in training camp at Santa Rosa, California, a few years back. Herock, who now scouts for the Raiders, had been working hard in camp and decided it was his night to break training. He deserved it. But the Raiders had a strict curfew during training camp, and Herock was trying to figure out how to beat bedcheck.

No doubt about it—he had a brilliant idea. He took the lamp from the nightstand, shade and all, and stuffed it under his bedcovers, fluffing the pillow at the top to make it look as if he was asleep. That way, he figured, if someone stuck his head into the room after curfew, he'd be fooled by the bulk in the bed.

There was only one thing wrong with the plan. Kenny forgot to unplug the lamp. When the assistant coach stuck his head through the door he reached over to flip on the wall light switch.

The bed lit up.

Readers of my first book may recall that my first spring training roomie was Jim Piersall, which prompted Angels manager Bill Rigney to say: "It was an easy decision. I didn't want to screw up two rooms."

It was Piersall, too, who said, "Don't blame me for Johnstone. He was crazy before I met him."

Needless to say, I looked up to Piersall, figuring

anyone who could chase down baseballs like Jimmy and still have enough energy to throw them against Bill Veeck's exploding scoreboard had to be something special.

My next Angels roomie was Joey Amalfitano, completely the opposite of Piersall. Joey would take me to dinner but he never said much and never bothered anybody. Joey was a gentleman—still is, for that matter. We got along well because he never said anything and I got to do all the talking. It was like having a room to myself, except that Joey always made sure we got to the right places at the right time. He even made sure I ate the right things so I'd have energy. In return, I made sure the room was clean.

Joey A. was a great example for a youngster like me, because he remembered all too well what happened when he was a 19-year-old bonus baby, required by baseball rules to remain on the major league roster all season. That's the year Leo Durocher's Giants swept the Cleveland Indians in four straight World Series games and Joey had a front row seat on the Giants' bench.

Amalfitano says he'll never forget pitcher Larry Jansen ordering him to drink champagne in the clubhouse after the Giants clinched the National League pennant.

"But why?" asked Joey. "I don't drink."

"Because you may never get this chance again," said Jansen.

Joey laughed. Never get this chance again? Who was Jansen kidding?

"But I'm glad he did that," Joey told me last summer. "I haven't been back to a World Series since as player, coach, or manager. And, believe me, 33 years is a long time between sips."

That Giants pennant celebration, incidentally, was apparently a doozie. Regular second baseman Davey Williams guzzled so much champagne that he slept that night in his locker, in uniform. That's where manager Durocher found him the next day, and Leo figured he'd have some fun.

"You're in the lineup, Williams."

"You gotta be kidding."

"You're my second baseman, aren't you? Get out there!"

Davey could hardly walk but Durocher made him play the first inning. Finally, after the third out, Williams lurched toward Durocher in the dugout and said:

"Who do you think I am, Lou Gehrig?"

That's when Leo relented and allowed the kid, Amalfitano, to play. It was one of only nine games Joey played during 1954 and his only appearance at second base, but he went on to log 10 years of major league service (and one brilliant stint as my roomie) before moving into the coaching box.

But I digress. My next roomie was Tom Egan, the first of a long line of catchers I had for roomies. Egan wasn't exactly what I'd call stable. Neither were the roomies to follow him, Clyde Wright and Rick Reichardt. We were all single in those days and our doors were never locked. Sleep? I don't ever remember getting any. But I made sure the room stayed clean.

Pitcher Jim Coates was a roomie of a different sort. A lot of guys didn't like him because he was always knocking them down. It seemed like I was always defending him, not that it did much good. Finally I said, "Geez, Rooms, I can understand you coming inside with a pitch once in a while, but do you have to knock down our own guys in batting practice?"

After that he would only throw sliders to me in batting practice. He wouldn't even say hello to people in the hotel lobby. He was tough on hotel inventories, too. He'd show up with two suitcases—one full of his clothes, the other empty—and he'd leave with a load of towels and bedsheets. He once gave Mary Jayne two sheets from a hotel and she made it into a curtain for our apartment. I wasn't overpaid in those days.

Another catcher, Joe Azcue, served his time as one of my roomies, as did Tom Satriano, who has become one of my closest friends, maybe because I could always beat him at gin. Every night we would play gin in the room, and every night he would lose. Then he'd get mad, throw the cards, and go to sleep. In the morning he'd pick them up so we could play again that night.

He never beat me, not once. The harder he tried, the more he lost. I could be staring out the window and draw a nine of clubs to an eight-ten-jack run. But he never held a grudge. We'd hit all of the Italian restaurants and all of the movies. But I never wanted him to overextend himself socially and get too tired. It's no fun to play gin against a guy who isn't sharp. Might change his game.

Ballplayers find fun where they can. When I was with the Angels, for example, it was a common occurrence for all of the guys on the team to be registered on the same floor of the hotel. I guess management figured that way the cops could handle any disturbances in one single sweep. On one road trip in Baltimore we found ourselves having belly-bumping contests at midnight. You could almost set your watch by it. One of the doors would fly open and the guys would begin corridor competition.

It was the midnight Olympics—guys hitting golf balls, having pillow fights, swinging at Whiffle balls, whatever. Belly-bumping competition, though, was the best: two guys would run toward each other from 30 feet away, hands behind their backs, bellies out, then collide. The one who went down was the loser, naturally. George Brunet was a champion belly-bumper. Bob Lee, Jack Sanford, and Lew Burdette held their own.

One of my favorite roomies, Tom Egan had one small problem. He would awaken in the middle of the night, positive that somebody was in the room. Usually it was me, but he was afraid it was an intruder. He'd jump out of bed in a cold sweat looking to punch somebody. There was no way you could sneak into a room where Egan was sleeping. He'd fly at you like Kato going after Peter Sellers in the old Pink Panther movies.

Being the compassionate and understanding teammates that we were, Clyde Wright and I decided to test Egan's reactions. One night, Clyde came tiptoeing into the room, but accidentally kicked a room service tray. That was all Egan needed. He knocked Wright over the tray and into the hallway. Another night Egan jumped up, grabbed the sofa, and threw it into the corner. It was always the same childhood dream—somebody was trying to get him. One night he was snoring so loudly, I pounded him with a pillow. He'd wake up, and I'd dash back to bed. Then he'd go back to sleep, start snoring, and I'd hit him again. This time, though, he didn't awaken, but the next morning he said he had dreamed about somebody beating him up. I never had the courage to tell him it was me.

We terrorized Egan. One night I waited until he went to sleep, then rang Melton and Herrmann in their room—just one ring, the prearranged signal— alerting them to come quietly to our room. Then the three of us took my mattress and fell on top of Egan. It was the damnedest fight you've ever seen. Egan came up fighting and kicking and scratching and it took three of us to hold him down.

Egan and I were roommates throughout my years with the White Sox. We still get together in southern California, but I don't know how he has been sleeping. Maybe I should slip over one of these nights and pound on his window.

Then there was Chuck Dobson, who I roomed with during my brief stay with the Oakland A's. It was like living with Attila the Hun. He'd stay awake half the night playing music, watching TV, never sleeping. With the Cardinals in spring training, though, I was luckier. I drew John Curtis, a left-handed pitcher who was always writing articles for magazines. He was a smart man and, let's face it, you didn't get many college graduates for roomies in the sixties and seventies. He spoke with a slow drawl and was always using the right words. I liked that and we became good friends, probably because he was so different and I was so normal.

Have you ever heard the story about the swimmer who cried "Shark . . . shark!" while his voice went from bass to soprano? Well, that's not the story I'm going to tell, but it's a good one. No, this story involves Mike Schmidt, my roomie one winter in Puerto Rico, and our brief adventure as scuba divers.

We must have spent $600 for equipment. We were

going to do the whole James Bond bit—swim down through the coral, meet mermaids, play with turtles.

So down we go, amidst all the tropical fishies in about 20 feet of beautiful, clear water and there, just below us, was a shark looking up at us.

Then we looked up, and there was another shark looking down at us.

We were underwater guided missiles. We swam through schools of fish, over sea urchins, past the coral—never touched a thing, we were flapping so fast—and the next day we sold all the equipment for half price.

I don't know about Schmidt, but I haven't been under water since, except for when one of my partners in my auto parts business ran off with all the money. But he was a different kind of shark.

Steve Yeager was the king of roommates. No ballplayer ever led a more active social life and survived. The Dodgers even had guards on him at night, but it didn't do any good. It was Yang, too, who helped me tie Lasorda in his Dodgertown room one night during spring training. We rigged a rope from his doorknob around a palm tree, and when he missed breakfast (he couldn't call for help because we'd rigged the phones, too), you'd have thought somebody had kidnapped Fernando Valenzuela.

Yeager, probably more than any major league player I've ever know, could relate to the common man. And uncommon women. Men like to hang around him at the bar and the women wanted to leave with him.

And, the last time I checked, he was still limping around major league diamonds with a surgical knee full of bolts and screws, playing hurt, firing strikes to second base, barking at young pitchers, and telling managers where to go and what they could do to themselves.

None of today's new players will have the experience of rooming with players like Yeager, Piersall, Egan, Satriano, or even Johnstone.

None of us made much money in those days, but we spent a lot of time together and became close friends. I guess the lack of money is why we needed each other. And I certainly suspect that the current availability of so much money and privacy explains why players spend so little time together nowadays.

And the next time some rookie wakes up in the middle of the night in Cleveland, Seattle, or some other foreign country, unable to conquer his nighttime fears, there won't be a roomie there to talk with him about it.

He won't have to worry about curfew, though. How can you order a player to be in at midnight when he owns stock in the hotel?

I always felt that I'd be very effective if I could go to the mound with a manager when things got rough for a pitcher. Lighten things up. Maybe go out dressed as a groundskeeper, tell the guy a few jokes, bring him a hot dog.

6

WHAT PITCHERS DON'T WANT YOU TO KNOW

I'm willing to admit that in my 22 years as a professional ballplayer, I've pulled off enough pranks and stunts to put Tom Lasorda *and* Danny Ozark into rubber rooms permanently. And I'm pretty sure that some of my teammates and managers haven't always appreciated my brand of humor. But I know this: if you're looking for the master tricksters in this business, don't look at me—look at the pitchers.

You know how it is with pitchers.

Pitchers have that spitball.

Now that I'm officially retired and no longer have to face spitballs (an Old-Timer wouldn't dare throw a spitter, would he?), I'm intrigued by the art.

A spitball, of course, isn't always necessarily a spitball. It can be a cutball, nickball, belt-buckle ball, dirtball, sandpaper ball, greaseball, petroleum jelly ball, whatever ball. Anything to make the baseball go crazy en route to the batter's box and send the hitter over the edge.

I love that old movie *It Happens Every Spring*, with Ray Milland playing the professor-turned-pitcher who carries a magic potion disguised as hair tonic that is allergic to wood, including baseball bats. Those celluloid hitters swing and the ball just hippety-hops over the bat. Great stuff. There's Jean Peters cheering on her hero from the stands, and the loyal catcher, Paul Douglas, who never understands why he can't pick up the ball with a splint on his finger. Then the manager, Ted De Corsia, unknowingly tries some of the gook on his wooden comb and his hair stands taller than Don King's.

Major league hitters who faced Jim "Mudcat" Grant can relate to that movie. Mudcat couldn't throw a spitter, but he developed a soapball. Before the game he'd take a bar of soap and lightly rub it into the front of his uniform shirt. He told me that it took him 30 minutes to do it properly, just to spread the soap around so it wasn't noticeable.

Then, during a game he'd wipe his forehead, neck, or anywhere else he was perspiring and, like a good little boy following baseball's rules, he'd "wipe off" the moisture by running his hand across his shirt.

He never got caught, but one day when it was extremely hot and he kept perspiring, he did have a problem.

Said Mudcat: "My shirt started bubbling."

Gaylord Perry, gentleman peanut farmer from Williamston, North Carolina, who won 314 games during 22 major league seasons, probably got more mileage out of his "is he or isn't he?" pitch than anyone. He drove umpires crazy.

Yet the men in blue were his friends, too. It became a never-ending game: trying to figure out where ol' Gaylord was hiding whatever he was hiding before he put it on the baseball. One ump was obsessed by the challenge and Perry enjoyed teasing him. He kept changing his movements: first he'd touch his cap, then his belt, then his sleeve, but the ump couldn't catch him.

One night after a game, Gaylord ran into the ump at a restaurant and the ump said, "Gaylord, I'm going nuts. You've got to show me where you put it. I promise I won't call it on you and I promise I won't tell anybody, but you've just got to show me!"

So Gaylord, being a good guy, relented.

"I've got this gold chain hanging around my neck," he told the ump. "And before I pitch I put it right in my Adam's apple. It's a great spot to hide it."

Now it's two weeks later and that same umpire is working home plate, Perry is pitching, and he's in a tight spot. But his chain is hanging outside his uniform and, with two strikes on the hitter, he pauses to finger the chain and stuff it back inside his uniform. Then he turns to face the batter, but he can't pitch because the umpire is laughing so hard he has to call time out. Finally, the ump knew what was coming—but he never called it.

I batted against and played with Perry (San Diego Padres, 1979), and he was the best. That's no knock at Phil (the Vulture) Regan because he was an artist, too. And Don Sutton can work sandpaper better then most carpenters.

Lew Burdette, now, was something else. I wouldn't exactly call what he did art. He was downright messy. He'd stand on the mound, chew tobacco, and spit into the dirt until he had his own little mudpies. Then when he was in a tight situation he'd call time, bend over to tie his shoe, and come back with a handful of goo. I swear that when he pitched you could see that shit flying all over the place. You'd walk back to the dugout needing a clean shirt. The problem, though, was that you were walking back to the dugout.

But back to Perry for a minute. When he played with Cleveland in the early 1970s, he also did TV commercials for a business with a familiar name, Gaylord's Discount Store. To do the commercials, they needed an umpire. So Perry paid one of the guys in town with the American League crew.

It was a simple enough script. The umpire would walk to the mound with the Indians' catcher, Ray Fosse, and say:

"Hey, Ray, where are you going tonight?"

"I'm going to Gaylord's."

"What do you mean?" the ump would say. "You see this guy all day and you're going to Gaylord's?"

"No—Gaylord's Discount Stores," Fosse would answer. "They've got great bargains."

Then the umpire would go to Perry, search him, turn to the audience, and hold up his arms to indicate he couldn't find anything.

Harmless fun, right?

Except that the day after shooting the commercial, Perry was pitching against Minnesota and the same umpire was working home plate. About the fifth inning, the Twins' manager says to the ump, "You've got to check what he's putting on that ball."

"Oh, no," says the ump. "Don't ask me to do that."

But he does, and Fosse walks along with the ump, the same way he did in the TV commercial they filmed a day earlier.

And, just like on TV, the ump checks Perry over,

can't find a thing, turns around, and throws up his arms, and returns to home plate.

Now Fosse, Perry, and the umpire are all laughing but they are the only three people in Municipal Stadium who know why.

This one I love. Gaylord was in spring training with the Atlanta Braves in 1981 when a prominent umpire approached him.

"I want to see you here tomorrow at 7 A.M.," said the ump.

Seven in the morning? Perry didn't know what to think but he'd always had success keeping umpires happy, so why change now? He showed up at 7 A.M., in uniform, and there was the umpire with his son. Nobody else was around.

"My son pitches in high school," said the umpire. "He's throwin' the ball good, too, but it's straight."

Then he puts on a catcher's mitt, sends the boy to the mound, takes a jar of Vaseline out of his pocket, and hands it to Perry.

"Now you show my kid how to throw that pitch."

Perry loved spooking other players with his spitball. Some of them would blame him for anything and everything. Bobby Bonds once let a ball slip out of his hands in the outfield and later blamed Perry for it. Claimed the ball was too slick to handle.

"I got Reggie Jackson thrown out of at least four games," Perry told me. "One day in Texas I struck him out on forkballs and he got so mad he took off his glasses and threw them at me. Then he threw his helmet. Then he threw his bat.

"Another time in Seattle he brought a bucket of water out for me. I told him I wasn't thirsty."

The unique thing about Perry, too, was that he played in both leagues—with the Giants, Padres, and

Braves in the National League and Indians, Rangers, Yankees, Mariners, and Royals in the American League.

That meant that a lot of guys who played with him later played against him.

"Yeah," recalls Perry, "like the time in 1975 when I went to play for Billy Martin in Texas. He had always been on my case for doctoring the ball, but now he comes to me and says, 'I was just kidding you, Gaylord.' So I said 'That's fine, Billy, I can accept that.'

"About three weeks later I'm pitching for the Rangers in Minnesota and Billy is about to get fired. He had already been fired by the Twins so he really wants us to win this game. We had a 5–0 lead when he runs up to me after the eighth inning, grabs the front of my shirt, and starts screaming, 'I don't want to see anything but greaseballs from you in the last inning!'

" 'That's fine,' I said, so I grease up pretty good and walk to the mound. Well, the first pitch gets away from me, like 10 feet over the catcher's head. So I cut down on the mixture and the next one only misses home plate by 6 feet. Then I look over at the dugout and Billy's coming out, madder than hell.

" 'What were on those first two pitches?' he screams.

" 'Billy, I'm sorry,' I said. 'I put too much grease on the ball.'

" 'Thank you.' said Billy, and walked back into the dugout. He just wanted to make sure I was following his orders."

Some guys are more careful about their spitball reputations than others. Joe Horner, for example, was pitching once in an All-Star game when he was a member of the Phillies. The manager was Gil Hodges and the bullpen coach was Joe Pignatano, both with the Mets. So when Hodges gives Horner the signal to come into the game from the bullpen, Joe tosses his warm-up jacket to Pignatano.

That's when a tube of petroleum jelly fell out.

"What's this?" said Piggy.

"Oh, nothing," said Horner, who stuffed it back into his jacket.

Now Pignatano goes into the dugout and shows Hodges what he's found. And, with the Mets and Phillies playing each other 18 times a season, you can bet that from that point, Horner was under surveillance every time he pitched against the Mets.

Now don't get me wrong. I'm not picking on pitchers. They're just a different breed. Listen, if you hang around with Jerry Reuss long enough, you come to know these things. They get on that mound and strange things start happening. Like the time Reuss was pitching an exhibition game for the Dodgers one late-winter day against USC. But before delivering the first pitch, he calls time out and motions for all the infielders to come to the mound. Then Jerry steps away from the group, looks into the audience, and says:

"You know, guys, there are 30,000 people up there right now and they're all looking at me. How does my hair look? OK? Does my uniform look neat enough?"

Then he takes off his cap, smooths back his hair, and just stands there enjoying the moment while the bewildered infielders shake their heads in amazement.

I always felt that I'd be very effective if I could go to the mound with the manager when things got rough for a pitcher. Lighten things up a bit. Maybe go out dressed as a groundskeeper, tell the guy a few jokes, bring him a hot dog. Just to break the tension.

Willie Stargell had the right idea in the seventh game of the 1979 World Series. Kent Tekulve is on the mound for the Pirates, leading the Orioles 2–1, two outs, bottom of the eighth in Baltimore. Eddie Murray, the switch hitter with awesome power, walks to the plate.

"I had been having trouble getting out left-handed hitters," recalled Tekulve, who has retired many hitters with his classic submarine pitch. "So I'm standing there and, frankly, I was sort of nervous. Then over walks Willie Stargell from first base. He looks at me and says, 'They tell me you have trouble with left-handers. Is that right?'

" 'Yeah, sometimes,' I said.

" 'Well, I'm left-handed,' said Stargell. 'How about you going over to play first base, I'll pitch to this dude, and we'll get out of this jam?'

"Well, I cracked up. I have to turn around and walk behind the mound and face center field because I'm laughing so hard into my glove.

"Eventually, I gain my composure, and get Murray to fly out to deep right field. We added a pair of runs in the ninth and we win the final game of the Series, 4–1.

"Now we're in Florida the following spring and Keith Jackson, who had been doing play-by-play for network television, comes to me and says, 'I've got to ask you this. We had cameras all over you in that seventh game, but nobody could figure out what you were laughing about.' So I told him the story and he couldn't believe that Stargell would make that kind of joke at that crucial moment.

"But I understood, because it took Willie just that one second to relax me and help me do my job.

"Then on Opening Day, 1980, I'm on the mound again with a couple of left-handed hitters coming up. I call Stargell over to the mound and say, 'Remember what you said to me in the seventh game? Well, if you ever do it again, I'm going to walk to first base and hand you the ball. Then you explain to Chuck Tanner what in hell is going on!'

"Willie never made any more propositions."

Can you imagine, though, someone like Bob Gibson acting like that? If you were to list all the funny things that ever happened with Bob Gibson on the mound, it would be the shortest list in history. Gibson wasn't out there for laughs.

As Gibson tells it, "When I pitched, I didn't think anything was funny."

Gibby didn't fool around because it wasn't his style. He not only intimidated fans, sportswriters, umpires, and enemy players—some of his own teammates walked softly as well. One thing about Gibby, though: they knew he played to win.

Yet, Gibson tells this one on himself and another Hall of Famer, Hank Aaron: "Hank never stole much and, frankly, I never had a real good move to first base. Still, I always tried to mix up a runner's timing so he wouldn't get a good jump off the bag. This time Aaron was on first base and as I came to my stretch, I looked over my shoulder and saw him sneakin' off, just waiting for me to kick my leg.

"But I didn't kick. I just held it until he got off, too far, caught between first and second, and I turned and ran right at him.

"I stayed about six or seven feet from him, looking him right in the eye. Everytime he'd go to the right, I'd go to the right, too. Then he'd move left and I'd move left, but I wasn't trying to tag him, just freeze

him. Finally, I said: 'I got your ass, I got your ass!' and
he started laughing so hard that he fell down, right
there in the base path.

"Then I tagged him."

Joe Torre, who has gone the distance in baseball as
a player, manager, and now announcer with the
California Angels, tells this classic story about
Gibson:

"All-Star Game, 1965, when I was still with the
Braves, and I was catching. Gibson was with the
Cardinals, of course, and our last pitcher in the game.
We were up in Minnesota and it's the bottom of the
tenth, and we're trying to hold a 6–5 lead. Tony Oliva
was the hitter, the crowd was going nuts, and I'm
saying to myself, 'It's an 0-and-2 count on this guy . . .
should I go out and tell Gibby to throw them up and
in, or should I just assume he's going to do that?'
After all, we all knew Gibby was a tough customer
and if you didn't play alongside him, pal, you didn't
talk to him. He was that tough.

"On the other hand, I figure why second guess
myself later? I'll just go out and remind him. So I
walk to the mound—remember now, the count is 0
and 2 on Oliva—and I say, 'Gibby, it's 0 and 2 so get
the ball up and in on Oliva, not down and in.'

"He just looked at me. He never said a word. Didn't
shake his head, nothing. Just looked. I felt naked out
there, so I hustled back to home plate as quickly as I
could, called the fastball, and waited.

"Well, sure enough—just to show me who's boss—
he throws it down and in. Oliva doubles. Then Gibson
strikes out the next three guys—wham, wham,
wham!'

"Now it's after the game, we're in the shower and I
say, 'Nice pitching, Bob.'

"He didn't even say 'Thank you.' He just ignored me.

"Yet, four years later I was traded from the Braves to Gibson's team, the Cardinals, in exchange for Orlando Cepeda. Gibson was the first man to welcome me into the clubhouse. And he said, 'When Bing Devine asked me if we should get Joe Torre in a trade. I told him, "Hell, yes!"

"But then he added, maybe just so I wouldn't get too friendly: 'But I told him not to give Cepeda for you.'"

Ever wonder what a pitcher and manager talk about on the mound? It's been a long time since Jim O'Toole stood on the pitcher's mound to argue with his manager, the late, and great, Fred Hutchinson, but O'Toole tells the story as if it happened yesterday.

It was 1961, the year southpaw O'Toole went 19–9 and Hutchinson's Reds won the National League pennant, and they were playing the Dodgers in Los Angeles. O'Toole had been superb. He was winning 3–0 with a shutout in the ninth. The first Dodger, though, gets a base hit, and the next batter grounds a twister between O'Toole's legs that Hutch felt his pitcher should have fielded. So the manager walks to the mound and, according to O'Toole—now an official Old-Timer at age 50—the conversation went this way:

"Don't take me out, Hutch. You know our bullpen is in trouble, so let me finish this one."

"Give me the ball, O'Toole."

"Hutch, there's no way in the world I'm leaving this game."

"I don't want any crap from you, O'Toole. Give me the goddamned ball!"

"Hutch, so help me . . . I'm finishing this game."

Well, the conversation continued for a few more minutes until home-plate umpire Jocko Conlan, unable to hold his laughter, came to the mound. Apparently he'd never heard anyone talk back to Hutch, who was not only big but strong. And standing around the Reds' infield were guys like Eddie Kasko, Don Blasingame, and Gene Freese trying to guess whether O'Toole would get fined $300, $500, $1,000, or lose his life.

Finally, Jocko goes back to the plate, but the argument resumes.

"If you want a part of my butt, Hutch, you can have it, but I'm not leaving this game."

"Give me the ball, O'Toole."

That's when Jimmy flipped the ball into the air, Hutch grabbed it with one hand, and dragged O'Toole off the mound with the other.

Bill Henry came into the game, but walked the bases loaded, and there was Duke Snider at the plate. O'Toole, meanwhile, was inside the clubhouse on his fourth beer, listening to the game on the radio. Duke fouls three into the stands, then finally flies out and the Reds escape.

By now, O'Toole has drained his sixth beer and greets Hutch as he comes into the clubhouse: "God, I'm glad we won. I acted like a damned fool out there, but I sure did want to finish that game."

Said Hutchinson: "Jimmy, if you weren't like that, I wouldn't want you on my team."

There was no fine.

Ok. But what would have happened if this was, say, the World Series? And what if the manager happened to be wired for sound by a network? And what if the manager also happened to be Tom Lasorda, whose vocabulary has been known to make truckers blush? Well, that's exactly what happened during Game

Four of the 1977 Series between the Dodgers and the Yankees. Lasorda, wearing a microphone to accommodate network TV, had just gone to the mound to remove pitcher Doug Rau from the game. Wisely, however, the network chose not to send this conversation into the nation's living rooms, because there were no "bleeps" in Lasorda's vocabulary that day— just the real thing. But I'll spare your ears:

LASORDA (to Rau): You can't get them bleepin' left-handers out, for bleep-all-bleepin' mighty.

RAU: Bleepin' Jackie, jammin' that bleepin' ball. I feel good, Tommy.

LASORDA: I don't give a bleep you feel good. There's four bleeperbleepin' hits up there.

RAU: They're all bleepin' hits the opposite way, too.

LASORDA: I don't give a bleep.

RAU: Tommy, they've got a left-hander hitting, I can strike this bleeperbleeper out.

LASORDA: I don't give a bleep, Dougie.

RAU: I think you're wrong.

LASORDA: Well, I may be wrong but that's my bleepin' job.

RAU: I ain't bleepin' hurtin'.

LASORDA: I make the bleepin' decisions here, OK?

RAU: There were three bleepin' runs on the board yesterday.

LASORDA (screaming): I don't give a bleep!

(Enter the voice of umpire Jerry Dale, who has joined Lasorda and Rau on the mound.)

DALE: Hey, hey, calm down.

LASORDA: I'm making the bleepin' decisions. Don't give me any bleep, Dougie. Keep your bleepin' mouth shut.

DALE: Hey, it's getting bad out here. Just back off the mound. You wanna talk about it, talk about it inside.

LASORDA (to Rau): We'll talk about it in my bleepin' office.

RAU: If I was pitchin' bad, I wouldn't say nothin'.

DALE: I'm just saying, talk about it inside. This is not the place to talk about it, OK? That's all I'm trying to say. I'm just trying to avoid a bleepin' scene out here, that's all.

LASORDA: That's right. It's bleepin' great for you [Rau] to be standin' out here talkin' to me like that.

RAU: If I didn't feel good, I wouldn't say nothin'.

LASORDA: I don't give a bleep, Doug. I'm the bleepin' manager of the bleepin' team and I gotta make the bleepin' decisions. And I'll make 'em to the best of my bleepin' ability. This may be the bleepin' wrong decision, but I'll make it. Don't worry about it, I'll make the bleepin' decisions. I gave you a bleepin' chance to walk out here, I can't bleep around. We're down two games to one. If this was yesterday it might be a different bleepin' story.

RAU: They got a left-handed hitter comin' up . . .

LASORDA: I don't give a bleep. You had three left-handed hitters and they all got bleepin' hits on you . . . Rivers, Jackson, and the other bleepin' guy . . . that guy who just hit the ball was left-handed, wasn't he?

RAU: I jammed him on the inside part of the plate . . .

LASORDA: I don't give a bleep whether you jammed him or not. He didn't get out. I can't leave you out here in a bleepin' game like this. I got a bleepin' job to do. What's the matter with you?

Fortunately for the network people, who by now were looking for a window to dive out of, Rau got the message and headed for the clubhouse. And I'm sure the episode ranks on his list of All-Time Embarrassing Moments. But even the greats have those incidents that make them want to crawl under a rosin bag.

Hoyt Wilhelm, for example, pitched 21 years for eight teams in the major leagues and was a deserving entrant into the Hall of Fame in 1985. He won only

143 games but that's not the point. He pitched in 1,070, and 1,018 of those were in relief. His knuckleball danced like a firefly while Hoyt just stood there, his head cocked to one side, seldom changing expression.

His entrance to Cooperstown, however, was not the result of his fielding. Wilhelm, now 63, recalls this doozie: "I was pitching for Atlanta in 1969 in Los Angeles—bottom of the eighth inning and we had a one-run lead, one out. There was a drive hit into the outfield, one run scored, and the winning run was coming into third base. I was backing up Clete Boyer at third, and how many ever get past him? Well, this one did. The throw hits the bag and ricochets right toward the dugout.

"God, I'll never forget it. I'm after that ball like a dog after a rabbit. I know the winning run will score if I don't get it before it goes into the dugout, so I make a very ungraceful dive, skid on my knee, and catch the ball just before it goes down.

"Then I come up to throw home, but the runner has fallen down rounding third. I don't realize this until too late, though, and as I'm throwing I'm also trying to stop. Well, I hold the damned ball, then it gets away from me and, if you believe it, bounces straight to Boyer at third, who tags out the base runner trying to get back.

"I've never been so embarrassed in my life, but we were out of the inning."

But back to Lasorda for a minute. Remember Kurt Bevacqua? Tommy hasn't forgotten him. He registered this opinion of Bevacqua after Kurt had suggested that Lasorda ordered a knockdown pitch at

Joe Lefebvre in a game between the Dodgers and San Diego Padres:

> I'll tell you what I think. It was very, very bad for that man to make an accusation like that. That was terrible. I have never, ever, since I've managed, ever told a pitcher to throw at anybody, nor will I ever. And if I ever did, I certainly wouldn't make him throw at a bleepin' .130 hitter like Lefebvre or bleepin' Bevacqua, who couldn't hit water if he fell out of a bleepin' boat. And I'll guaran-bleepin'-tee you this, when I pitched and I was gonna pitch against a bleepin' team that had guys on it like Bevacqua, I sent a bleepin' limousine to get the bleepbleeper to make sure he was in the bleeperbleepin' lineup, because I'd kick the bleep-bleeper's bleep any bleepin' day of the week. He's a bleepin' bleeperbleepin' big mouth, I'll tell you that.

Do you get the idea that Tommy doesn't appreciate having his integrity questioned? Actually, there's more to it than that. He has a certain passion for pitchers, because he was one himself back in the mid-1950s, when he appeared with the Brooklyn Dodgers for four games in 1954 and four games in 1955 and with Kansas City for eighteen games in 1956. His lifetime ERA is 6.48. Yet he had a hard time figuring out why the Dodgers cut him in 1955. It infuriated him that he was being released for some young kid.

It didn't matter to him that the kid's name was Koufax.

Dodger batboys received a crash course in bizarre behavior in 1986. They watched in amazement as Reuss filled Ken 'Buns' Howell's suit trousers with ice while Kenny was outside running. And during one particularly boring game, they watched a young lady seated behind home plate go into a strip tease act.

7
THOSE DREADED DODGER BLUES

I never had the opportunity to play for Walter Alston, but the boys who did tell me that his doghouse was not one to visit.

Bill Russell, now a coach with the Dodgers, visited it once because of mistaken identity.

It was one of those warm spring nights in Vero Beach, Florida, where the Dodgers train, and Billy was returning from Lenny's, a saloon near Dodgertown, with teammate Steve Shirley. But as they were walking along the nine-hole golf course that adjoins the training facility, they noticed a golf cart hanging halfway off the bridge, with the bridge's handrail running directly through the middle of the cart.

Russell and Shirley were convinced that somebody must have been seriously injured, but they couldn't find any survivors. They were worried about missing curfew and getting blamed for the cart. So, like good little Dodgers, they reported their find to Dodger officials Guy Wellman and Bill Schweppe.

That was not, however, the end of the story. Alston got the news one day later that two of his players "found" a damaged golf cart on the way back from Lenny's. He was not particularly pleased about it.

"For the next two years Alston kept reminding me I should get a license for driving golf carts," said Russell. "And I'll swear to this day that it wasn't me. But I don't think he ever did believe me."

I believe you, Billy, because I know who wrecked the golf cart.

It was Bobby Castillo and Bob Welch. They were coming back from Lenny's, too.

Hey, so they made one wrong turn. Nobody is perfect, especially at Vero Beach in the springtime.

As I said, I regret that I never played for Alston, but I am grateful for the years I played with the Dodgers, particularly because one of those years, 1981, brought me my second World Series ring (my first one came in 1978 with the Yankees), and another year, 1985, saw us win a division championship. And I got the chance to revolutionize Lasorda's life. Some of my best material came from those Dodger years.

But I have to confess that I'm impressed by some of the stunts that have gone on behind the scenes there in my absence. Let's face it—when things aren't going well for a team, that's the time to toss in a little humor. So I have to tip my hat to the guys who pulled off this escapade, all at the expense of one Steve Sax.

It all started innocently enough with another free lunch for Tom Lasorda and invited guests at his brother's restaurant outside Philadelphia. It was an afternoon before a night game—plenty of free time

and festivity, right down to the roasted pig with an apple in its mouth to be expertly carved by the Dodger manager himself.

There was no particular plan. But the guests all just sat there looking at this beautiful pig with a funny look on his face and an apple in his mouth, and it could not be wasted. So when lunch was finished, batboy Jon Scott and Dodger coach Mark Cresse got a plastic garbage bag from the kitchen, packed the piggie (well, actually, only the head), and took it onto the bus back to the Franklin Plaza hotel, where the Dodgers were staying.

Now what to do with it?

Everybody came up with the same suggestion: Steve Sax. Traveling Secretary Billy DeLury got an extra key to the second baseman's room while Lasorda called Sax on the phone.

"You'd better get down here," said Lasorda, even though the team bus wasn't scheduled to leave for another two hours. "I want to talk to you about something."

Sax, who wasn't having much of a season in 1985, figured he was being traded.

So while he was coming down the elevator, Cresse, Scott, batboy Mitch Poole, and bullpen catcher Todd Maulding went up the fire stairs, opened Sax's room, put this gorgeous pig head into the bed, and covered it.

When Sax returned after his meeting with Lasorda, however, he didn't notice the pig. Only Steve Sax would not notice a pig in his bed. He caught the bus, played the game against the Phillies, and returned to the hotel later that night.

He still didn't notice. He didn't even smell anything, and it had been there almost 12 hours.

Saxy just got into bed, watched television for at

least an hour, then reached across the bed for the light switch.

That's when he screamed.

Attached to Mr. Pig was an anonymous note: "You'd better start bearing down out there or else. The Godfather."

Sax was so shaken that he changed rooms, and the following day he asked trustworthy batboy Scott to accompany him to his room ("Just check the bathroom, will you, in case somebody put a snake in there"), never dreaming that young Scott had been one of the porker planters.

To this day Sax has blamed Lasorda and Reuss. Now he will learn differently. Never trust anybody in a baseball clubhouse. Not even the guys who shine the shoes.

Batboys Poole and Scott have received a crash course in bizarre behavior at Dodger Stadium during the past few years, particularly in 1986, when things weren't going so well for the Dodgers. They watched last summer with amazement while Reuss filled Ken "Buns" Howell's suit trousers with ice while Kenny was outside running. They witnessed three fans during a game race from their box seats in right field to second base, give the bag a twirl, then race back to their seats and the arresting officers. And during one particularly boring game, they watched a young lady behind home plate go into a strip tease act.

"Awesome job," said Poole.

"Bitchin'," said Scott.

Then closing day finally arrived and, although the Dodgers were to finish just a half-game out of the NL West cellar, there was one final attempt at good humor, if not originality.

Four Dodger players—Rick Honeycutt, Jack Fimple, Ed Vande Berg, and Larry See—decided it would be a good day to imitate groundskeepers. So, following the footsteps of Reuss and yours truly, who had lit up the DodgerVision board a few years earlier with our groundskeepers act, this fearsome foursome put on coveralls and went through the entire routine.

There was only one problem.

Nobody noticed.

It was that kind of year for the Dodgers.

Lasorda should have suspected it was going to be rough when Commissioner Peter V. Ueberroth ruled during the spring of 1986 that all clubhouses would be off-limits to celebrities, jewelry salesmen, agents, hangers-on, etc., and, unfortunately for Lasorda, that rule also applied to his Dodger Stadium office. My poor pal Tommy was left alone to look at all of those pictures of Frank Sinatra and Don Rickles by himself. I disagree with the rule and think it should be amended to "friends only" in the manager's office. I'm convinced that the Dodgers slipped in 1986 because Lasorda was lonely. He even might have missed *me*.

There was the tip-off, too, in spring training when Lasorda was taken to jail and nobody would bail him out. It was one of those charity fundraisers in Vero Beach, and Dodger sportswriters couldn't resist. They had Lasorda arrested—the squad car with flashing red light took him right off the practice field—and bail was set at $1,000.

I am very sorry that I had nothing to do with this one.

From jail he called Dodger vice president Al Campanis. He wouldn't pay. Then he called the clubhouse man, Dave Wright. He wouldn't pay either. None of the players would chip in a nickel, even after Tommy had been incarcerated, in uniform, for four hours. He knew by then, of course, that it was all for charity and he was entertaining everybody in jail. But he was also getting the red-ass because nobody would put up the $1,000.

Finally, entertainer Danny Kaye, who was visiting Dodgertown, bailed the manager out of jail.

There are those who contend the season went downhill from there.

Seriously, you really can tell when things are going badly for a baseball team. You'd be surprised at all of the uncomfortable things that can happen to a loser. "Snakebit" takes on a new meaning.

Stu Nahan, a radio-TV sportscaster in L.A., tells this true story: "I park my Mercedes at the supermarket for 10 minutes, that's all, just 10 minutes, and when I come out it's gone. So I take my bag of groceries to a nearby police car, report the theft, and they drive me home. They've got my wallet so I have to cancel credit cards, and they've got my cellular phone so I have to make sure somebody isn't out there calling Honduras on my number.

"Later that afternooon, though, I get a call that my car has been found. The credit cards are missing, the phone is gone, everything in the trunk is gone, even the license plates have been taken.

"But the rotten thieves left one thing. I had Dodger season tickets on the front seat, and they didn't touch them."

That's when a team knows it's doing badly.

Nahan's favorite Lasorda story: it's 10:50 P.M. in Vero Beach during spring training. For Lasorda, that's a significant time. Others may be partaking in stronger stuff at Bobby's on the Beach, the Ocean Grill, Tahitian, Uptown, or any of the other watering holes along the Atlantic Ocean, but Lasorda is a Swenson's man. He loves his ice cream, and he knows that Swenson's closes at 11 P.M..

"And on this night he's running late," tells Nahan, "so he loads a group of us into his car, and we drive like hell for Swenson's. Well, we get there at 10:58 P.M., some guy is stacking chairs upside down on the tables, and Lasorda is hot.

" 'I want a hot fudge sundae!' he yells through the door.

" 'The boss is out back,' says the guy stacking chairs.

"Now Tommy walks around behind the building into a driveway and there's a parked car that's moving like there's an earthquake. I mean this car is vibrating!

" 'I'm going to see what's going on,' says Lasorda.

"Hey," I said, "we're in redneck territory. Let's just go back to Dodgertown."

Instead, Tommy pulls open the door and there, on the front seat, are two employees of Swenson's, a male and a female, and they're rather busy.

" 'Hi, Tommy,' says the guy, pulling up his trousers.

" 'I want to get four hot fudge sundaes,' says Lasorda.

" 'Just a minute,' says the guy, and he tosses Lasorda the keys to the building.

"Lasorda closes the door, the guy resumes his friendship with the lady, and we go inside for ice cream. Now picture the scene: there's Lasorda, making four hot fudge sundaes—whipped cream, cherries on top, nuts, the whole business—and he's mad.

" 'Can you imagine, he says, 'that that guy wouldn't stop what he was doing to serve us?' "

Sorry, Stu, but if you think that's Lasorda being mad, you haven't tuned into some of his postgame "chats" with the press. One of my favorites came after Dave Kingman hit three dingers off Dodger pitching in one game. And someone made the mistake of asking him his opinion of the performance:

LASORDA: What's my opinion of Kingman's performance? What the bleep you think is my opinion of it? It was bleepin' bleep-bleep. Put that in . . . I don't bleepin' . . . opinion of his performance? Bleep bleep. He beat us with three bleepin' home runs. What the bleep do you mean what is my opinion of his performance? How can you ask me a question like that, what is my opinion of his performance? Bleep bleep, he hit three home runs. Bleep bleep. I'm bleepin' bleeped off to lose the bleepin' game. And you ask me my opinion of his performance, bleep bleep. I mean that's a tough question to ask me, isn't it? What is my opinion of his performance?

REPORTER: Yes, it is. I asked it and you gave me an answer.

LASORDA: Well, I didn't give you a good answer because I'm mad, but that's a tough question to ask me right now. What is my opinion of his performance? I mean you want me to tell you the opinion of his performance? Bleep bleep! The guy hits three home runs against us. Bleep! I mean, I don't mean to get bleeped off or anything like that but you know you asked me my opinion. He put on a helluva' show. He hit three home runs. He drove in what, seven runs?

REPORTER: Eight.

LASORDA: Eight runs. Well, what the hell more can you say about it? I didn't mean to get mad or anything but bleep bleep! You asked me my opinion of his performance?

Well, I wish I could repeat it for you *exactly* the way he said it, but with my reputation for getting banned, I thought it best to use a few judicious bleeps instead. Also, Lasorda is still good for a free meal now and then, and I don't want him mad at me.

But while I'm at it, what about this scorcher from Lasorda a few years back when Scott Sanderson was on the mound for Montreal, and he destroyed the Dodgers:

I ain't bleepin' bleepin' you when I say this. That bleepin' bleep-bleeper, he was buryin' himself right on the mound and we're swinging at balls bleepin' high. He walked Russell, he don't come close to the bleepin' plate. He walks Sax, he don't come near the bleepin' plate. Now two balls and one bleepin' strike and a bleepin' ball up in his bleepin' eyes and Landreaux is wavin' at the bleeperbleepin' ball. How the bleep can you hit that bleepin' guy? Garvey needed a bleepin' oar to hit the bleepin' ball tonight. That's how bad those bleepin' pitchers were. He'd a-made a great bleepin' cricket player, hittin' 'em on one bleepin' bounce. I'll tell you it's a bleepin' crime. We had more bleepin' scoring opportunities to win that bleeperbleepin' game and I'll tell you, them bleep-bleepers get away with that bleepin' bleep, them bleeperbleepers! Bleep 'em, lucky bleeper-bleepers [sounds of kicking]. How the bleep do them bleep-bleepers get by with that bleepin' bleep? [More kicking]. Put that in your bleepin' paper, T.J. [Terry Johnson, *South Bay Breeze*, Los Angeles]. Every bleepin' word I said. Put it in the bleeperbleepin' paper. I don't give a bleep, T.J.!

Answered the astounded reporter: "How do you spell [sound of kicking]?"

You really can't blame Tommy for getting a little hot now and then. After all, look at some of the players he's had to contend with—even if you take Jerry Reuss and me off the list, you still have a whole clubhouse full of characters who are slowly but surely sliding over the edge.

Steve Sax, for example.

You had to see Lasorda's face the time Sax ripped a double, stumbled rounding first, then collapsed after rounding second. Lasorda and trainer Bill Buhler, obviously concerned, rushed to the fallen player.

"Where did you get hurt?" asked Lasorda.

"Over there," answered Sax, pointing back to the first base line.

Lasorda loves to tell stories about Sax, although I'm not sure they're all true.

"Sax came to me complaining that he couldn't sell his old car because it had 100,000 miles on it," says Lasorda, "so I told him, 'roll back the speedometer and nobody would know how old it was.'

"Well, about a week later I saw Saxy and I asked, 'How much did you get for that car, Steve?'

" 'Oh, Skip, I didn't sell it, I kept it. Why should I sell a car with only 10,000 miles on it?' "

"

I always kept a special lookout for nuns in the audience. If I saw a nun, I'd go up into the stands in uniform, sit with her, and ask for a little divine guidance. There was a streak when it seemed like every time I did something for a nun, I'd hit a home run. I was running around doing everything but passing the collection plate.

"

8
FLYING PANTIES AND OTHER HAZARDS

It was the late Si Burick of Dayton, Ohio, one of the more beloved sportswriters of our time, who wrote about the removal of exotic dancer Morganna from a baseball field by four security men:

"And so they escorted her off the field, two a breast."

Morganna and those like her—although there are few *quite* like Morganna—are still as much a part of major league baseball in the 1980s as was Hilda, the gravel-voiced lady of Flatbush who rang cowbells for the Brooklyn Dodgers of the 1940s.

It would be inaccurate, of course, to compare Morganna and her flopping whatevers with Hilda and her clanging bells. Morganna wants publicity and gets it. Hilda wanted her Bums of Brooklyn to win!

Perhaps a more typical and true fanatic of the

eighties would be someone like Dodger Mom, the lady who parks her car first in line at the entrance gate of every Dodger home game, opens the door, and sits there in a flowery muumuu sewing or reading while waiting to wave to the players as they arrive at the ballpark. Then there's Chicago's extraordinary Ronnie "Whoooo," a young man with cast-iron lungs who hovers around the visitor's clubhouse entrance at Wrigley Field in Chicago. He knows all the players and managers from all the enemy teams and can shout and heckle with the best ("Lasorda, WHOOO . . . Lasorda, WHOOO . . . Lasorda, WHOOO!").

Again, no harm, no foul. But Dodger Mom and Ronnie wouldn't make the prelims in New York, where there are fans of another feather. One of the favorites with visiting players is the lady known only as New York Red. She always sits by the bullpen and tries to make dates with the players. She knows the name of every relief pitcher in baseball and maybe even a few other things about them.

Ahh, New York fans. They had pitcher Ed Whitson of the San Diego Padres so squirrelly during the 1986 season that he refused to step onto the Shea Stadium field. Whitson had played across town with the Yankees earlier in the season and received death threats. And after being traded to San Diego, he simply refused to pitch at Shea. He showed up in New York wearing sunglasses and wouldn't walk the streets. "Walking out there at Yankee Stadium was like carrying a bullseye on your back," said Whitson about his days as a New York player.

He may have gotten spooked, too, after a customer threw a knife out of the upper deck during the 1986 season and grazed the arm of rookie Wally Joyner of the Angels. Wally, needless to say, was surprised.

Nobody had thrown knives at him when he played at Brigham Young University.

Actually, he and Whitson probably overreacted. Surely that fan wasn't throwing the knife *at Wally*. He was probably just trying to stab and rob the person next to him and the knife slipped.

Did fans ever throw things at me? Sure, all the time.

Bras and panties, mostly.

I'm serious.

At the height of my popularity in Philadelphia, in the mid-seventies, I had a real love affair with the people in the outfield stands. I was involved in a lot of public service and promotional things throughout the Philly area, too, and frankly, I made a point of keeping the fans on my side.

I'd throw baseballs into the crowd and bubble gum to the kids, trade baseballs for a Coke or a hot dog. I called it "playing money," and I'd simply turn to the crowd and say "OK, I've got a baseball here ... who'll give me what for it?" and we'd make a swap.

Giving away baseballs got me into a little trouble once with the Dodgers in San Francisco. I had this box of autographed balls all ready to give away, but somebody stole it. I don't know who took it, it just disappeared. That gave me the red-ass so I went into the clubhouse, came back with *four boxes* of balls and threw away every baseball into the audience.

That made Lasorda furious. He screamed, "How can you do that? How can you throw away all our baseballs? Now what are we going to use?"

He had a point. So, proving that two wrongs can indeed make a right, I walked across the diamond to the dugout of the Giants, who had gone inside for a team meeting.

I stole four boxes of *their* baseballs and they never did figure out what happened to them.

People were always throwing things. I'd sign them and throw them back.

Yes, bras and panties. Hey, it's better than signing a knife.

I always kept a special lookout for nuns in the audience. If I saw a nun and had time before a game, I'd walk up through the crowd in uniform, sit with her, and ask for a little divine guidance. It never hurt, and after a while, I got superstitious about it. There was a streak in Chicago with the Cubs when it seemed like every time I did something for a nun, I'd hit a home run. Man, I was running around doing everything but passing the collection plate.

In Philly, too, there was one particular Sister who couldn't get to the games very often, but whenever she showed up, I almost always did well. Then one day I got this letter: "Dear Jay, I haven't been to the park because I've been very sick, but I've been reading about you and just wanted to tell you we're all behind you." Well, on the day I got the letter, I hit a home run. I couldn't get back to the locker room fast enough.

"Dear Sister," I wrote, "Get well quickly. You gotta come out here . . . I need you."

I guess that's why I've always been puzzled by ballplayers who have problems with fans, even in New York. I just think that if players put out a little effort, they can bring the fans to their side.

As for throwing things, that's another problem. Booze has a lot to do with it. Control the sale of beer—cut it off after the seventh inning, for example—and you can control the audience behavior. At Dodger Stadium they quit selling beer in the outfield pavilion area during the mid-1970s when the Dodgers and Cincinnati Reds were such rivals. Fans in L.A. figured the Big Red Machine—particularly an outfielder named Pete Rose—needed lubrication, so they threw everything from beer to ball bearings until beer sales were stopped. Then the throwing also stopped, and it was no coincidence.

I will give L.A. fans a point for originality. Once an airplane dropped a bag of flour, which landed near Maury Wills at shortstop. If it had landed on him, he would have been killed. On another occasion, a bag of rocks and garbage fell from Dodger Stadium's upper deck and landed near the backstop.

I guess they didn't have any bras and panties up there in the red zone.

Mets fan Michael Sergio of Manhattan also scored a point for originality during the first inning of Game Six of the 1986 World Series when he parachuted onto the Shea Stadium infield. Sergio landed between the pitcher's mound and first base and was quickly escorted off the field by police officers. That didn't bother me as much as wondering how the private plane that carried him above Shea managed to maneuver through all that commerical air space.

Do you think Morganna ever considered parachuting onto a field? Incredible concept.

I can understand, though, why some fans do bizarre things at ballparks. Why not? I made a career out of it. Baseball can get boring, especially if it's a bad game. And if it can get boring *during* a game, what about *between* games?

I remember sitting around massage parlors for excitement. I was playing with the Toledo Mud Hens in 1974 while waiting to be called into the majors by the Phillies. Jim Bunning was my manager, and my roomate was a goofy catcher named Harry Safewright.

Harry and I loved to terrorize Bunning, who took himself much too seriously in those days, so we'd spend our evenings on the road going to massage parlors, which were popular in those days.

But we didn't go for the massage. We just liked going there because the foyers usually had cable TV and we could see programs we couldn't get in the hotel room. So we'd go to Charleston or Richmond or another of the exotic Triple-A cities, and our idea of a perfect evening was to go to White Castle for a bag of burgers, then take the burgers to a massage parlor and watch TV.

We'd just sit there in the lobby, occasionally making remarks to the customers as they departed, and I never could figure out why they didn't have us arrested. I guess they figured we provided entertainment.

Bunning was always hoping to catch us at something, so Harry and I were always dreaming up practical jokes to curdle his stomach. Example: We'd let it be known around the clubhouse that we were going to a wild party that night with booze, girls, all-night music, the whole bit. We'd make a big deal out of it.

Then that night we'd stay in our hotel room and, sure enough, Bunning would open our door with a key he had gotten from the front desk. But instead of finding an empty room or a party, he'd find Johnstone and Safewright sitting on the bed playing cards.

"Hey, Jim, nice seeing you," I'd say. "I didn't know you had a key to our room. Wanna play some gin?"

Then he'd throw the key and slam the door.

It took him almost a full year to understand me before we became good friends. Jim has since turned to politics, and I'm hoping he becomes the governor of Kentucky, his state. I don't even want to think about the fun I could have with that.

Pretty sick humor, huh? Well, it gets that way sometimes when you've got some time to kill, especially in the minor leagues. Pat Corrales, manager of the Cleveland Indians, tells about the time he was in Triple-A with Lee Elia. They'd go into an airport with one of the players in a wheelchair—not hurt, just faking it under a blanket—and about halfway down the concourse, the chair would tip over and the guy would fall out.

Then the other players would fake kicking the guy lying on the floor and yelling for him to get back in his wheelchair. "Get up!" they'd shout. "And don't you ever fall out of that chair again." Then somebody would kick him again and he'd just lie there moaning while bystanders watched in horror.

Usually they wouldn't stop until somebody called the airport police. Then the guy would pop up, give the cop a grin, and spin down the corridor in his wheelchair.

Very sick humor. And I'm a little upset I never thought if it myself.

Sick humor? Al Hrabosky, once the Mad Hungarian and now a television announcer in St. Louis, which isn't a lot different, has been over the edge on a number of occasions.

Once he took a hand grenade into the clubhouse.

It was 1978, his first with the Kansas City Royals after a successful career with the St. Louis Cardinals, and I guess Al figured he needed to establish his personality. The Royals had gotten off to a poor start so one day the Mad Hungarian walked into the clubhouse and said: "Look, you sons of bitches, if we don't get our act together and start winning, they're going to blame this on me and I ain't taking it alone. I ain't going down alone—I'm taking some of you suckers with me, so pay attention. This here's a hand grenade I'm holding and if we go bad, I'm pulling the pin and blowing all of you to hell and back!"

He then placed the hand grenade in his locker and walked out.

It was a very effective speech. Half the guys didn't know whether to believe Al or not because, after all, he was mad. Anyhow, the Royals finished strongly to win their division. Now it's celebration time and Hrabosky reaches suddenly into the locker and grabs the hand grenade.

"I knew you guys would come back and save me!" yells Al, who finished the season with 20 saves and an ERA of 2.88.

But now he pulls the pin and, so help me, guys start diving for cover.

"Don't worry!" yells Al, "I'm holding the pin. I'll hold it down if I can. Oh, shit, it's bent—hey, somebody help me straighten this! Quick, get me some pliers!"

Finally, he places the grenade back in his locker and everybody is laughing at their crazy relief pitcher.

The next day, though, somebody from the Royals' front office calls Hrabosky on the phone.

"Al," he says, "I know this is going to sound ridiculous, but we got a call from somebody who said you threatened to blow up the clubhouse."

"What do you mean?" asks the innocent Hungarian.

"Well, somebody told me you threatened to pull the pin on a hand grenade."

"Yeah, I did," says Al, and hung up.

The grenade, of course, had long ago been disarmed.

I think.

Hrabosky, though, didn't get his nickname without earning it. Once in Wrigley Field, after a night on the town with the boys, he decided to wear his uniform a little differently in the bullpen.

He wore his protective cup and jockstrap on the outside of his pants.

For six innings, he sat in the bullpen in full view of the audience with his jock on the outside.

"I knew what I was doing," said Hrabosky. "They never need me until the eighth or ninth, anyhow."

After a few years in the majors, you learn to find creative ways to pass time on road trips while waiting for a night game. You can only watch so much cable TV. Chris Speier and Chris Arnold, for example, got their kicks one day while wandering around the old Shamrock Hilton hotel in Houston, Texas, that place with a swimming pool large enough to float a battleship. They were teammates with San Francisco then, and, let's face it, the Giants needed laughs any way they could get them.

So it's one of those how-do-we-kill-time afternoons before a night game in the Astrodome between the Giants and the Astros, and Speier and Arnold are meandering through the Shamrock lobby when they hear music. Being curious sorts, they walk into a huge ballroom and see a group of entertainers onstage rehearsing a musical number. Speier decides that this looks like fun so they walk to the front of the auditorium and take a seat.

"We figured we'd just listen to them jam a while," said Speier.

That's how it began.

"Oh," says one of the entertainers, spotting the two well-dressed vistors, "is one of you Mr. Erickson?"

"Yes," says Speier, his senses alert.

"OK," says the entertainer, "we're ready to start."

"Well, go right ahead," says Speier.

So now the music starts, tap dancers go into their routine, and a dozen singers in the back row start harmonizing. Speier and Arnold, meanwhile, are paying serious attention and talking quietly to each other.

"Well," says the group's leader, after the number was finished. "What do you think?"

"I'll be honest," says Speier. "It's going to be a pretty young crowd in here and I think your costumes are a little blasé. Do you have anything you could wear to spice it up a bit?"

"Oh, yes . . . sure, sure," the leader says and the whole group disappears to change clothes.

Now they return and the girls are wearing a lot less and looking a lot better to the ballplayers.

"Could you run through that last number again?" asks Speier.

"Oh, yes, Mr. Erickson," the leader says.

"I wonder who in hell Mr. Erickson is?" whispers Arnold.

"Damned if I know," says Speier, settling back to check out the girls' costumes.

The group does the entire act again and by the finish they're huffing and puffing, waiting for approval.

So where is it written that ballplayers can't hang out at the
concession stands during a game?

My humble beginnings: it was a long time before the kid in the
front row, far right, gave his first hotfoot.

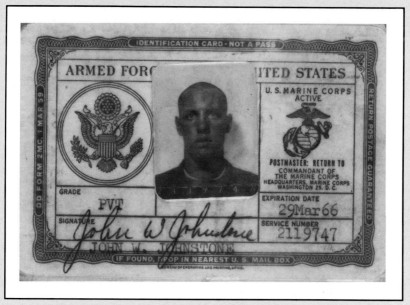

The ultimate lean, mean fighting machine.

Tupman Institute of Technology

Upon the Nomination of the Faculty and the Board of Regents ·
has conferred upon

John William Johnstone

the Degree of
Doctorate of History

Given under the Seal of the University of Tupman in the
State of California on this sixth day of June in the
year Nineteen hundred Seventy-six.

Secretary of the State Board

President of the University

You've heard of UCLA? USC? MIT? Well, I got my honorary
degree from TIT. And I don't know if it has a baseball team.

Danny Ozark never knew where to find me, but it's hard to
stay hidden when the scoreboard keeps blowing your cover.

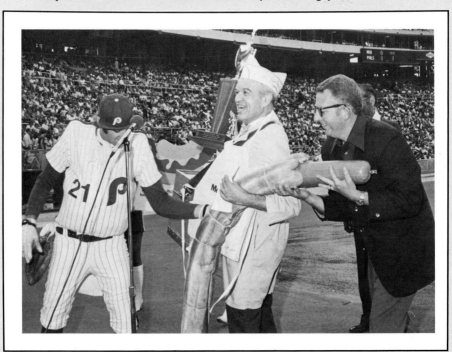

Veterans Stadium's famous hot dog man was the proud
recipient of the biggest hot dog ever made, presented by Phils
president Bill Giles on the right and "The Old Man of
Baseball" on the left. I don't even want to guess what he did
with the thing.

I never could hit a changeup. And I'm not sure if this one ever came down.

This is Chicago's famous statue of General Sheridan, and his horse's famous derriere. The scaffolding is there because workmen were actually removing paint from the affected area, but you can guess how long it stayed clean.

Why does anyone bother arguing with an umpire? Yogi and I tried here, but you know it didn't help. And they call this a democracy.

That's the tough thing about being a ballplayer—beautiful women always want to have their pictures taken with you.

The Life and Times . . .

. . . of an Outfielder

The Garv.
He does great things
for my image.

The thrill of victory after winning the World Series in 1981.
Two seconds later, Valenzuela dumped that whole bottle of
champagne on Steve Howe and me.

It was sunny when this game started, but in Wrigley Field, you never know what's coming.

Ernie Banks was trying to tell me what a great hitter he was, but how can you believe a guy whose idea of "great" is to play two games?

If you read *Temporary Insanity*, you know that this is the infamous strongman routine. It wouldn't be polite to reveal the helpless victim's identity, but that's Rick Sutcliffe doing the honors (with a little help from coach Mark Cresse and me).

If Tommy finds me, I'm dead.

Don't let these smiling faces fool you—I've always taken the blame for the havoc Garvey and Reuss have caused.

At the Phillies' Old-Timers Game, none of the old catchers could walk anymore, so I did the honors.

When you win, you're allowed to look like this. (A word about Tom Niedenfuer's hat: he earned it and his nickname, Buffalohead, because he has to wear a *huge*—size eight— helmet.)

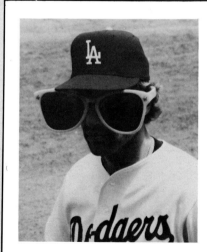

That's the last time *I'll* lose a fly ball in the sun. . . .
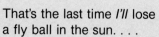

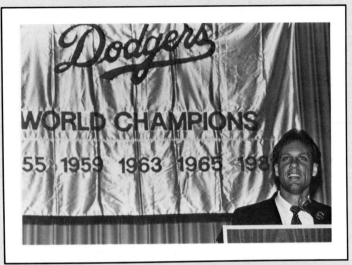

I was glad to speak at this Dodger luncheon, but I took a poll of the audience and we all agreed we'd rather be someplace else.

"Forget about the sign . . . just pitch the damn ball!"

No one could stop Lou Brock when he was playing,
but now that he's an Old-Timer, even *I* can catch him.

Steve Sax and I spent all
day with this guy before we
realized he wasn't Lasorda.

Senator Garvey and I entertained at *Sports Illustrated*'s 1986 World Series bash in New York. Actually, I entertained. Garvey practiced his campaign speeches.

What am I doing with all these Old-Timers? I just wanted to show the guys what it's like to be able to move across a dance floor.

My new broadcasting career is exciting, but the headset always messes up my hair.

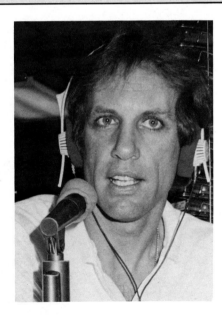

The Equitable Old-Timers Team: (Front row, L to R): Bill "Moose" Skowron, Bill Melton, Luis Tiant, Paul Blair, Joe Torre, Willie Davis, Willie Horton, Dave Cash. (Back row, L to R): Jay Johnstone, Jim Lonborg, Jim Perry, Jim "Mudcat" Grant, Gaylord Perry, an Unknown Blue Jay, Eddie Mathews, Tom Tresh, Ernie Banks.

My buddy, Daryl Brilliant.

Talk about Old-Timers—Niedenfuer and I helped Elliott Gould with his game during our magnificent performance in *Faerie Tale Theatre*'s "Casey at the Bat."

JAY JOHNSTONE'S LIFETIME STATISTICS

YEAR	CLUB	AVG.	G	AB	R	H	2B	3B	HR	RBI	BB	SO	SB
1963	San Jose[1]	.252	48	155	21	39	5	3	1	18	10	45	3
1964	San Jose[1]	.291	126	454	66	132	27	11	4	48	39	81	13
1965	El Paso[1]	.285	35	137	21	39	9	2	1	21	13	11	1
	San Jose[1]	.301	97	356	53	107	17	6	6	60	26	21	9
1966	El Paso[1]	.360	7	25	5	9	2	0	1	1	3	3	0
	Seattle[1]	.340	81	318	60	108	14	7	7	42	16	31	11
1967	California Angels	.264	61	254	35	67	12	4	3	17	11	36	3
	California Angels	.209	79	230	18	48	7	1	2	10	5	37	3
	Seattle[1]	.315	49	184	21	58	11	1	4	21	7	17	2
1968	California Angels	.261	41	115	11	30	4	1	0	3	7	15	2
	Seattle[1]	.277	84	314	45	87	15	4	13	56	22	47	4
1969	California Angels	.270	148	540	64	146	20	5	10	59	38	75	3
1970	California Angels	.238	119	320	34	76	10	5	11	39	24	53	1
1971	Chicago White Sox	.260	124	388	53	101	14	1	16	40	38	50	10
1972	Chicago White Sox	.188	113	261	27	49	9	0	4	17	25	42	2
1973	Oakland A's	.107	23	28	1	3	1	0	0	3	2	4	0
1974	Tucson[2]	.347	69	242	58	84	15	5	9	44	30	26	4
	Toledo[3]	.316	57	155	31	49	15	1	8	25	24	25	2
	Philadelphia Phillies	.295	64	200	30	59	10	4	6	30	24	28	5

YEAR	CLUB	AVG.	G	AB	R	H	2B	3B	HR	RBI	BB	SO	SB
1975	Philadelphia Phillies	.329	122	350	50	115	19	2	7	54	42	39	7
1976	Philadelphia Phillies	.318	129	440	62	140	38	4	5	53	41	39	5
1977	Philadelphia Phillies	.284	112	363	64	103	18	4	15	59	38	38	3
1978	Philadelphia Phillies	.179	35	56	3	10	2	0	0	4	6	9	0
	New York Yankees	.262	36	65	6	17	0	0	1	6	4	10	0
1979	New York Yankees	.208	23	48	7	10	1	0	1	7	2	7	1
	San Diego Padres	.294	75	201	10	59	8	2	0	32	18	21	1
1980	Los Angeles Dodgers	.307	109	251	31	77	15	2	2	20	24	29	3
1981	Los Angeles Dodgers	.205	61	83	8	17	3	0	3	6	7	13	0
1982	Los Angeles Dodgers	.077	21	13	1	1	1	0	0	2	5	2	0
	Chicago Cubs	.249	98	269	39	67	13	1	10	43	40	41	0
1983	Chicago Cubs	.257	86	140	16	36	7	0	6	22	20	24	1
1984	Chicago Cubs	.288	52	73	8	21	2	2	0	3	7	18	0
1985	Los Angeles Dodgers	.133	17	15	0	2	1	0	0	2	1	2	0
	American League Totals	.243	767	2249	256	547	78	17	48	201	156	329	25
	National League Totals	.288	981	2454	322	707	137	21	54	330	373	303	25
	Major League Totals	.266	1748	4703	578	1254	215	38	102	531	429	632	50

1California Angels—minor league
2Oakland A's—minor league
3Philadelphia Phillies—minor league

Mary Jayne, my bride of twenty years.

Mary Jayne Sarah made our home team complete.

"I hate to say this," says Speier, "but this is a big hall and we're going to have 500 to 600 people here and I'm really afraid they're not going to hear everything. Isn't there anything you can do with the stage to get better resonance?"

"Oh, yeah," says the leader, "we can put down some plywood."

So this time they build a little plywood stage for the tap dancers, who once more do their routine.

"Fantastic," says Speier, when they finish. "That was perfect. We're going to have to discuss this with our manager but as far as we're concerned, you've got our vote. Just wait right here and we'll be right back."

And just as Speier and Arnold are departing the ballroom, a man named Erickson walks in.

"OK, places everybody," he yells. "Let's take a look at this act."

Ballplayers and entertainers have a special affinity, and I'm convinced that most actors harbor fantasies of being professional athletes. That's why celebrity games are always so successful. There is never a shortage of entertainers ready to chase down fly balls.

Hollywood Stars Night, for example, is always a successful promotion at Dodger Stadium. Where else can you find Kareem Abdul-Jabbar hitting line drives to left center or Robin Williams sliding into home plate?

The late Danny Goodman, member of the Friars' Club and for years the concessionaire at Dodger Stadium, started Hollywood Stars Night back in the late 1950s when the Dodgers still played in the Coliseum. Jerry Lewis and Dean Martin loved it. So did Jackie Gleason and Sammy Davis, Jr. Nowadays you can see Telly Savalas, Billy Crystal, or Mark Harmon trying to turn a double play or reach the fences.

My favorite Hollywood Star is actor Billy Barty, the midget, and he helped me sting one of my all-time targets, Ron Cey, a.k.a. the Penguin.

I showed up several hours before the Hollywood Stars game, which was scheduled ahead of a regular Dodger game, and worked out the details with Barty. We appropriated Cey's uniform out of his locker, put it on Barty, and placed him at third base, wearing number 10.

Surely you've seen Billy Barty. He's hardly tall enough to see over third base, let alone play it. On the other hand, Cey may be listed as 5'10" but can't be taller than 5'6". Well, maybe 5'7".

Anyhow, there was Barty at third base when Cey showed up at Dodger Stadium. But before he could scream about his uniform being gone, I brought Barty into the dugout and said:

"We've got to find a different uniform for Billy. This one he's got is too tight."

After all, aren't ballplayers entertainers anyway? Aren't we out there to show the fans a good time (aside from winning games, of course)? Fans can make or break a season (would San Diego have won the pennant in 1984 without them?), and they can sure break a player. Ever sit out in the left-field bleachers at Wrigley? Those wonderful Bums can drive a visiting fielder over the edge and then some, because they're only about 20 feet from the action. I hope knife tossing never catches on there.

I talk a lot about how much I love the fans, and it's true. That's why you'll often find me up in the stands—maybe I even sold you this book. I'd much rather talk baseball in the stands than hang out in the dugout with a bunch of sweaty guys and a manager who keeps watching me over his shoulder.

So even though I'm out of the game now, you can still find me roaming around ballparks. After all, you can never sign enough panties and bras. And you never know when Morganna is going to drop in.

And it beats killing ants.

" It took Steven Patrick Garvey 19 years to get thrown out of a game. When I first heard the news, I said, 'No way . . . there must be some mistake. They must mean Gene Garber or maybe it was Doug Harvey. It can't be Steve Garvey. What did he do? Say 'gee, golly, gosh' too many times?

9
IF RODNEY DANGERFIELD PLAYED BASEBALL

EIGHT WAYS TO GIVE A THIRD-BASE COACH ULCERS

1. Act like you can't hear him.
2. Give him the "I don't understand" sign.
3. Make him keep repeating the sign from the coaching box.
4. Run through his stop sign.
5. Tell him he's giving the signs too fast.
6. Tell him he's giving the signs too slow.
7. When he gives the take sign, swing away.
8. When queried by the manager, say "What sign?"

I love third-base coaching stories. Other than being in the broadcast booth, where you get to talk all of the time, I think the third-base coaching box would be the next best place to spend an evening at the ballpark. You've got a great view of all the action, you can visit with the umpire, fans, third baseman, guys in the dugout, and occasionally a base runner. Mostly, though, it's a no-brainer; you just stand there yelling "Hey baby, hey baby," toss in a few "atta-boys," and then flap and slap your arms around like you're being attacked by killer mosquitoes. That's the job.

On a good day.

On a bad day, these guys get no respect. They're totally unappreciated, overlooked. Because while you're watching the action and guessing whether or not the runner is going, the base coach is sweating bullets wondering if the runner *knows* whether or not he's going. Take this story from my ex-roomie Joey Amalfitano, who came up as a bonus baby with the New York Giants in 1954 and has remained in the majors ever since, spending 33 years as a player, coach, and manager. He now coaches third base for the Los Angeles Dodgers.

When this weird scenario took place, though, he was coaching for the Cubs, those delightful northsiders from Chicago who haven't won a pennant since the end of World War II.

No, Joey wasn't with them in 1945, but on this particular windy day in May 1979, the Cubs and Phillies were staging their own version of war. The Phillies eventually won, 23–22, on Mike Schmidt's home run off Bruce Sutter in the 10th inning. This was the game, too, in which the Cubs sent Sutter, Willie Hernandez, Bill Caudill, and Donnie Moore, among others, to the mound in relief. None of them got the job done that day, yet all four went on to sign lucrative contracts and find success with other teams later in their careers.

Anyhow, Joey was coaching third during the middle innings and the Cubs were trailing 17–6. A real tight one. They've got runners on first and third, though, with nobody out, so things are happening. That's when Amalfitano "suggests" to the runner on third base, Mike Vail, that he should go home on any kind of ground ball. Joey's logic was sound: leading by 11 runs, surely the Phillies would go for a double play and concede the run at home plate.

"Remember, Mike," Joey reminded Vail, "go home on any ground ball—and if you do get hung up at home plate, make sure to get caught in a run-down long enough to advance the other two runners."

Amalfitano knows, however, that the odds are 100 to 1 against the Phils throwing home. They just want a double play to move the game along.

So, sure enough, Dave Kingman grounds into a double play—shortstop to second base to first.

But Vail doesn't budge from third base. He turns instead to Amalfitano and says: "You didn't want me to go on that one, did you?"

"Actually, I did," says Joey, "but I think it's a little late now." Earth to Mike, and Joey is wondering if anyone would notice if he just stuffed Vail under the bag.

The next hitter was retired, the Cubs failed to score and eventually lost by that run Vail failed to score, 23–22.

Now it's six months later—the dead of winter in Chicago—and although Joey isn't losing sleep anymore over the play, the WGN television executives decide it would be a good time to rebroadcast the 23–22 game. After all, there isn't a lot to do in Chicago during the winter except eat, drink, and wait for spring training. So WGN showed the game and it was a ratings smash. Masochistic Cub fans were able to snuggle up near their fireplaces and suffer all over again. It was wonderful.

Watching the game, too, was a gentleman in Florida who had cable TV. And when he saw Vail standing on third base while a double play was being completed, he was aghast. He immediately wrote a scathing letter to Amalfitano, in care of Wrigley Field, asking, "How dumb can a coach be, not sending home a runner in that situation? No wonder the Cubs never win with guys like you working for them!"

What did I tell you? Totally unappreciated.

Joey took it personally, but what could he do? Fans, after all, are entitled to their opinions, misguided as they might be.

The following summer—more than one year after the 23–22 game—Joey is having lunch in Atlanta one game day with another coach, Billy Williams, when a man walks up and starts talking with Williams, using the standard I've-been-a-Cub-fan-all-my-life routine.

"What did you say your name was?" asks Amalfitano.

The fellow tells him again and bells start ringing in Joey's head. "I thought I recognized that name," said Joey. "You wrote me a letter. Now let me answer it!"

No, Joey didn't punch the guy. He didn't even dump a salad on him. He did, however, explain why some athletes are better suited to play baseball than become brain surgeons. He got his payback, although I'm sure he would rather have had a shot at Mike Vail.

And, believe me, Joey has paid his dues as a coach—some of them quite painful, actually. Like the time in 1985 when Steve Sax homered (it was his one and only dinger that year) and was so pumped up as he rounded third that he gave coach Joey a low five that was sort of like a karate chop. He fractured Joey's thumb.

I've freaked out a few coaches myself. Sometimes, you know, your concentration lapses. Like Ken Landreaux, who played with the Dodgers throughout the early 1980s. I've seen K.T. stare right through a third-base coach—as if the guy wasn't even there. And the poor coach is flapping away like a wild bird trying to get his attention.

Not that the Dodger signs are that complicated. Once Lasorda gave a "go" sign to Landreaux, through the normal chain of cammand, and it went like this:

Lasorda, in the dugout, flashed a sign to third-base coach Amalfitano, who sent it along to first-base coach Manny Mota, who gave it to baserunner Landreaux.

But nothing happened. Landreaux didn't go. So on the next pitch Lasorda sent along the sign, via Amalfitano, to Mota, to Landreaux.

Same result. Nothing. Lasorda is fuming in the dugout and Mota, wanting to make sure K.T. gets the sign, walks over to first base, gives Kenny a huge wink and returns to the coach's box.

Landreaux still doesn't go and the hitter grounds into a 6-4-3 double play.

Now Lasorda is screaming at Amalfitano when everyone returns to the dugout. "What happened?"

"I don't know," said Joey, "I gave the sign to Mota."

"What happened?" Lasorda screams at Mota.

"I don't know," said Manny. "I not only gave him the sign, I winked at him."

"Then what happened?" asked Lasorda.

"He winked back."

Sometimes giving signs is less complicated than it

looks, however. Consider this incident with the 1980 Philadelphia Phillies:

Lee Elia was in the third-base coaching box (his date with destiny with the Chicago Cubs still three years away), but I won't identify the base runner on third. He's too sensitive. Anyhow, Elia walks up to this Phillie and says, "Now, listen, I'm going to say your last name if the squeeze is on. I'll say your last name. Don't pay attention to anything else I say. Just listen for your last name, OK?"

"OK," says the runner. No problem, right?

So he takes his lead off third, listens carefully, and sure enough, he hears his name! The squeeze is on. But, as the pitcher goes into his stretch—just to make sure—our friend turns to the coach and shouts:

"Now?"

So what can Elia do? He shouts back:

"Now! Now! Go!"

Incredibly, the squeeze play worked anyway.

Bobby Wine remembers how he got to meet the press while coaching third with the Atlanta Braves in 1985. On this particular night, Wine was coaching third against the Pirates, and the Braves had been playing like sleepwalkers, trailing by one run in the ninth. An Atlanta runner reaches second, however, and Gerald Perry rips a line drive into right field, where the outfielder tries a shoestring catch and misses the ball. Wine waves home the runner, looks up to see Perry storming around second, and gives him the "whoa" sign. Unbelieving, Perry stops, even though he probably could have gotten an inside-the-park home run. Then he really can't believe his eyes because there goes Wine trotting off the field.

"I thought we had won the game!" said Wine. "I had completely forgotten the score."

"I could have won the game," yelled Perry.

"I know that now," apologized Wine.

Luckily, Chris Chambliss followed with a base hit, Perry scored the winning run, and Wine was off the hook.

But he got to meet the press, anyhow.

You see, most coaches remain anonymous unless they screw up. If a third-base coach goes the entire season without being interviewed after a game, it means he had a perfect season.

The sad thing is that people tend to completely overlook these guys. There they are, with fractured thumbs and the like, trying desperately to control a crazed runner from plowing into the dugout, or trying to flash signals to a space cadet out in the ozone. And yet their success is measured by how obscure they can be. Can you blame them for feeling unappreciated?

Well, guys, you're not the only ones. When it comes to being unappreciated, you're not even at the top of the list. I could tell you about the trials of being a pinch hitter—standing around for seven innings trying to look important—but even pinch hitters get a *little* respect.

No, I'm afraid when it comes to being unappreciated, you've got to tip your hat to those charming men in blue, the umpires. Unloved, unrespected, unnoticed. Well, they *hope* to go unnoticed. The only time anyone notices an umpire is when there's a player or a manager kicking him in the shins.

So I'm here to tell you that some of these guys are all right with me.

Two of my favorite umpires in baseball are still punching them out at high speed in the National League—Bruce Froemming and Dutch "Pee Wee" Rennert. I've known Froemming since he was umpiring in the minor leagues 21 years ago, when I was with Seattle, the Angels' Triple-A farm club. Both Bruce and I, in fact, were waiting then to be called into the major leagues.

We had one great argument, too, and all because I was just trying to be helpful. I was trying to be *appreciative.*

I hit a ball into the dirt at home plate and it bounced back up. So, being a good guy, I reached out, grabbed it, and handed it back to the home plate umpire, who was Froemming.

"That wasn't foul, it was fair!" yelled Bruce, and he called me out for interference.

Then my manager, Bob Lemon, charged Froemming and said, "You're not in the Texas League now, you're in the Coast League."

"Yeah," said Froemming, "and you're in the Coast League with me!"

Bruce and Bob never did get along well after that. Froemming told me later that the game had been his first game in Triple-A after being promoted from the Texas League. He figured it was his last stop—either get promoted to the majors or quit umpiring.

"So why couldn't you have just run to first base like anybody else?" he asked me.

I don't know. I was just trying to be friendly. But I guess umpires aren't too accustomed to such radical behavior.

Oh, and about Pee Wee Rennert. Maybe you know him as Dutch. I'm the only player who ever called him Pee Wee and it still bugs him. Just by accident, I found out from a boyhood friend of his that Pee Wee had been his nickname as a kid.

Now, let's face it: no umpire with a macho nickname like Dutch wants to be called Pee Wee, right? So every time I'd get around him in games I'd call him Pee Wee. And, every time, he'd get mad. It never failed. Unfortunately, the name never caught on and I'm sure Pee Wee figures that since I'm out of baseball, he's safe.

That's why I wrote about it in this book. No umpire should ever feel absolutely at peace.

Another of my NL favorites is Eric Gregg, the occasionally plump ump who learned his trade in the Dominican Republic in 1973.

"That's where I met Tom Lasorda," recalled Gregg. "And when I had visa problems—and I mean serious problems—it was Lasorda who made a phone call and got everything fixed in 20 minutes.

"Now it's one year later and I make a call against one of Tommy's players, Bobby Valentine. So what does Lasorda do? He comes screaming at me and says, 'Eric, you can't call him out! I got you a visa!' "

Eric remembers his first game as a major league ump—September 26, 1975, Padres vs. Reds, in Cincinnati. He was working second base and scared to death.

"I'm so nervous I want to scream," said Gregg to the second baseman.

"Hey, be my guest, scream," came the answer.

So Gregg started screaming.

Now he's counting calories, along with a few other NL umps, because they've been catching heat from the league office. In truth, they have been threatened with expulsion from the majors unless they meet certain weight standards.

"When they start judging my work by my weight," says Eric, "I have just one question:

"How are the skinny guys doing?"

Some people may think that the weight issue is pretty important, but if you ask Dave Concepcion, he'll tell you that communication is a much weightier problem.

Poor Davey got into an argument with Dave Pallone at Wrigley Field in 1984 when I was with the Cubs. Davey went berserk and got the thumb, but the next day, when I asked Dan Driessen what it was all about, he said:

"Davey was calling him a cab."

"A cab? He called him a cab? Why would he get kicked out for calling him a cab?"

"Well, it sounded like he was screaming 'cab.' "

Nope. That was just Davey's Venezuelan accent. He was really calling Pallone a "scab" because he was one of the four umpires who got his job by working while the regular NL umps went on strike in 1979. Only two of those four remain in baseball today— Pallone and Fred Brocklander. And there is still a certain bitterness from many umpires directed at Pallone and Brocklander.

Davey proved you don't have to curse to get ejected—just mention one of those little buzzwords that make an umpire's thumb start to twitch.

Steve Garvey certainly learned *that* lesson the hard way. I promised Garv I was going to make it through this whole book without telling a story about him, but it wouldn't be my book if I couldn't give him a hard time. I have to tell you this story, simply because of its historic relevance to the world of baseball.

You see, it took Steven Patrick Garvey 19 years to get ejected from a game.

When I first heard the news that he had been

kicked out of a game, I said "No way ... there must be some mistake. They must mean Gene Garber or maybe it was Doug Harvey. It can't be Steve Garvey. What did he do? Say 'gee, golly, gosh,' too many times?"

Apparently he didn't say much more, proving once again that you don't have to curse to take an early shower.

In Garvey's case, he wasn't even involved in the play made at Jack Murphy Stadium by home-plate umpire Charlie Williams. Garv had been standing in the on-deck circle and had an excellent view of the sliding Bip Roberts, who ran his outstretched hand over the plate. TV replays indicated Roberts was safe, too. Williams, the ump, however, said the hand was *above* the plate during the slide and therefore only *appeared* to touch the plate.

Anyhow, Garvey stepped in, he and Williams began arguing, and then Williams suggested that Garvey had no business being there and that he was showing him up.

Garv, meanwhile, was drawing marks in the dirt with his bat to indicate where the slide had been made.

"I warned him to quit drawing circles like that," said Williams.

Garv, though, made another neat little design and said, as he turned to leave, "You gotta bear down, Charlie."

Goodbye, Senator Garvey. Charlie gave him the thumb.

Now when a *manager* tells a *player* to bear down, it's meant to motivate him. Maybe that's what Garv intended to do, motivate Charlie. But all he succeeded in doing was driving Charlie to the brink of hysteria. Imagine being shown up by the future President of the United States.

But it didn't end there. As if Charlie hadn't taken enough abuse, the next day Padre manager Steve Boros decided to offer his own brand of instant replay, and when he brought out the lineup to umpire Williams, he also brought with him a videotape of the controversial play. And good night to you, Mr. Boros. How 'bout a nice early shower?

Joe Pepitone was perhaps the ugliest American ever to wear spikes in Japan. He batted just .163 for 14 games, offended many Japanese with his long hair, after-hours behavior, and crude mannerisms, and suddenly returned to the United States complaining of injuries. One journalist suggested that Joe's premature baldness was his 'weak point' and caused psychological problems.

10
LAND OF THE RISING FUN

The Japanese word for individualism is *kojinshugi,* and I'm afraid that's why I never would have made it in Nippon.

I flirted with the idea toward the end of my career. I even had Alan Meersand, the agent who has signed more players to Japanese baseball contracts in the last decade than anyone, make inquiries.

The Japanese, however, aren't too keen on practical jokers. They don't call it the Land of the Rising Fun. My *kojinshugi* would have gotten me into big trouble. They're into "groupthink" in Japan and they have a proverb that applies to their baseball: *The nail that sticks up is hammered down.*

They could have done some fancy hammering on me. Can you imagine me walking onto a ballfield with my uniform under a kimono? Or trading a *besuboro* to a fan for a bowl of rice?

Frown is not a strong enough word for how the

137

Japanese feel about egocentric behavior that could disrupt a team.

Yet I am intrigued by baseball in Japan, mainly because of conversations I've had with Americans who played there. Some of their stories are amazing.

Many Japanese apparently don't want Americans over there at all. Each year you hear talk about American players being banned, and yet, they keep signing new ones. And the Americans who do perform for Japan's 12 professional teams—six in each league—face the ever-present conflict: The Japanese want you to succeed to help their team, but they also want you to fail because you're an American.

Consider Randy Bass, the most successful American baseball player ever in Japan. He recently signed a three-year contract worth $3.25 million with the Hanshin Tigers of Osaka. That makes him the highest-paid player in Japanese history. The only other $1 million player in Japan is ex-Montreal outfielder Warren Cromartie.

Bass, still just 32, has won two consecutive triple crowns in Japan: in 1985 he hit .350 with 54 home runs and 134 RBI, and in 1986 he hit .389 with 47 homers and 109 RBI.

Yet on the final day of the 1985 season when Bass was bidding to tie the legendary Sadaharu Oh's all-time record of 55 homers, consider what happened:

The Tigers were playing the Tokyo Giants, by far the most popular team in Japan, who were being managed by—you guessed it—Sadaharu Oh, their retired home-run hero.

When Bass came to the plate the first time, he had to lunge across the plate and throw his bat to hit a single. Then, with Oh watching impassively from the dugout, Bass was intentionally walked the next four times he came to the plate.

"It's probably best I didn't tie Oh's record," said Bass, when he returned to the United States during the off-season. "It would have been considered sacrilegious."

But Bass has been extremely popular in Japan, not only because of his hitting, but because of his "attitude." He doesn't say *bakayaro* ("you stupid son of a bitch") to umpires and, in the words of one observer of the Japanese game, he has been "reborn, forgetting that he ever played the game in America."

But he's still a *gaijin*—a foreigner with bat and glove from a strange land—and that's something that will never change.

Davey Johnson, manager of the world champion New York Mets, offers insight into playing in Japan perhaps as well as anyone can. Davey became the first non-Oriental to wear the uniform of the fabled Yomiuri (Tokyo) Giants in 1975, and he was given a record $120,000 two-year contract. He had hit 43-homers in 1973 in Atlanta and the Japanese expected him to take the place of their retired hero, Shigeru Nagashima.

Davey, though, had a slow start: he had lost 25 pounds, broken a bone in his shoulder, and had to adjust to the managerial quirks of Nagashima (retired heroes quickly become managers in Japan). When he hit .197 with 13 homers and the Giants finished last, Johnson became the scapegoat. One newspaper even wrote his name as J-*son*, and *son* means "loss" in Japan.

"When I first got there they wouldn't play me," recalls Johnson, "because they said I wasn't ready. I *wanted* to play, but that didn't matter. You have to understand Japanese philosophy. If you start badly, they figure you'll finish badly. I remember one game when I struck out in my first at-bat, I ran to my position, only to find another Japanese player already taking ground balls. They had made a change.

"Language is always a problem. So is diet. I went down to 165 pounds, and after that Japanese kid broke that bone in my back I missed six weeks.

"My second year was really an experience. The only thing that saved me was that I was over 30 years old. If you were over 30, you got to ride in a bus from training camp back to the hotel. If you were under 30, you had to run and it was four miles! We'd train for about three months—we'd train to the point of exhaustion, actually—dawn until dark most of the time. I've never seen anything like it."

Johnson tells about his celebrated run-in with Nagashima (maybe Davey should've taken a lesson from me and tied him in his room like I did to Lasorda), and understand this about Nagashima: until Oh, he was unquestionably the most popular player in Japanese history. Nicknamed the "Burning Man" because of his "fighting spirit," he played 17 seasons, won six batting titles, and hit 444 home runs before retiring to become manager of the Giants in 1975.

"Midway through my second season," said Johnson, "I got a bruise on my thumb, a knot from swinging at those inside fastballs, and it was so tender I could hardly swing. Nagashima insisted I keep taking batting practice, even thought it made it worse.

"Then they sent me to a doctor in downtown Tokyo and he pulled out this eight-inch needle that he wanted to stick in my neck, of all places, for one hour a day, 10 days straight. And that was going to heal my thumb.

" 'No way,' I said. I wanted to fly back to Los

Angeles to see Dr. Robert Kerlan, then return to Japan. I figured I just needed a cortisone shot from somebody who knew what he was doing. But we were in first place at the time and they wouldn't let me go.

"Finally, I just told Nagashima, 'I'm going to L.A. to get this fixed.' Then I walked off the field and went upstairs to shower and go to the airport. But as I'm coming out of the shower, Nagashima walks up to me, rips the towel from around my waist, points to my privates, and screams, 'That's a lie!'

"Well, I was infuriated. I didn't need Nagashima telling me I had no balls. So I flew to L.A. and Kerlan told me I had an inflamed nerve. He gave me a shot, told me to wear a cushion on the hand, and to go lightly in batting practice. Unfortunately, I couldn't go straight back to Tokyo because I had a 10-day visa delay, but I played in the first game after returning and hit a grand-slam home run to win the game.

"The Japanese were amazed. They simply couldn't understand how anybody could do that without practicing for 10 days."

And even though Davey went on to have a good season (26 HR, 75 RBI, .270), there were still problems. First he hit the home run in Hiroshima to clinch the pennant for the Giants (Oh had homered to tie the game) and he was a hero.

"But we had a workout the day before the Japan Series was to open," said Davey, " and it was raining and cold. We were diving for balls in the mud while photographers took our pictures—you know, good show, good fight, and all that—and the next day I had strep throat. I had to have penicillin and I had a high fever, but they begged me to play. Well, I struck out twice in game one and hit two long fly balls. I went 0 for 4 and we lost. The next day I struck out my first time up. So as I'm walking to the plate the second time, they send out a pinch hitter. That was it. I'd had it. Even after I was healthy and feeling better, they didn't use me for the rest of the Japan Series.

"That's when I decided to return to America. I figured if they didn't understand that a ballplayer has a lot of pride and that just because he strikes out the first time up, that doesn't necessarily mean he's going to have a bad day, then Japanese baseball wasn't for me. I've kept in touch, though, with the friends I made in Japan. Nagashima is a wonderful man, he really is, and I certainly don't criticize the quality of baseball over there. It's really excellent. The thinking is different, that's all."

And speaking of different thinking, Davey tells this one on the very different Clyde Wright.

"My funniest story: Clyde Wright was pitching for us during my second year and Clyde was a little strange anyhow. The Japanese called him Crazy Wright-o. Anyhow, he's pitching a shutout, 4–0, in about the fifth inning and I boot a ground ball for an error. Then the next guy gets a base hit and out to the mound comes this interpreter in a business suit, along with the pitching coach. They were making a pitching change because two men were on base and Clyde had given up one hit.

"Well, Clyde went nuts. He storms off the mound screaming that he's going to call the commissioner, that he's going to call Peter O'Malley, that he's going to tell everyone how badly Americans are treated in Japan. Then he throws his glove at the screen and starts tearing his uniform off in the dugout. Now he goes into the clubhouse and when somebody starts to take a picture of him he grabs the camera, can't figure how to get the film out, so he trashes the camera. He's tearing up his locker and yelling about calling O'Malley.

"Well, finally, to calm him down, the general manager starts apologizing and asking what he can do to keep him from calling the commissioner in America.

" 'Give me a $25,000 bonus!' screams Wright, and that's exactly what they did. They gave him $25,000.

" 'Geez,' I told Clyde afterward, 'I'm sorry I didn't boot two ground balls. Maybe you would have gotten $50,000!' "

Wright, a southpaw from Tennessee who threw a no-hitter with the Angels back in 1970 when he won 22 games (I played flawless center field that night), now operates a pitching school for boys in Anaheim. He also has vivid memories of playing in Japan:

"Other teams, particularly the Taiyo Whales, were always throwing at Davey," said Wright. "God, they loved to throw at the Americans. They'd walk the best Japanese hitters but they'd hit Davey in the ribs. Finally, one night we're playing the Whales and I said to Davey, 'This shit is gonna stop.' So when the first Japanese kid came to the plate I threw one behind his head. Actually, I was aiming at him but missed. Now my Japanese catcher won't even go into a crouch. He's just standing back there. I look over at Davey and say 'I'll get that son of a bitch if I have to throw a dozen at him.' Now I fire another one—splat! It hits right in the back of that kid's thin plastic helmet and plastic is flying everywhere.

"They never hit Davey again, and I think he hit 12 home runs off them that season."

The Japanese never quite understood Crazy Wright-o. There was a famous wire photo of him in 1978 arguing with an umpire—Clyde had pulled his cap bill down tightly over his nose so he could peck the ump with it.

"I kept calling him a little Chinese cocksucker," said Wright. "They get insulted when you call them Chinese.

"The thing that really got me, though, was one time some of the guys on my team were yelling at an American on another team and they're screaming, 'Yankee go home ... Yankee go home' and I said, 'Hey, guys, I'm a Yankee, too!' So whenever we'd get into any kind of argument, I'd just call them Chinese. It always pissed them off."

Wright, who earned a top salary of $87,500 in Japan before returning, admits he never could quite figure out the Japanese mentality.

"They'd bench a hitter if he had a poor batting practice," said Wright. "If a guy was hurt and wanted a day off they wouldn't give it to him. But if he was smart he'd just miss a few in batting practice and they'd take him out. Hell, it was the only way to get out of the lineup. Once I was in the bullpen warming up before starting a game and there was this Japanese teammate—a reliever—warming up right next to me. I said, 'What's he doing?' and my interpreter said, 'Oh, it's just in case the first two hitters get on base.'

"We had a guy in spring training who was having trouble catching fly balls. So what did they do? They had somebody hit him 1,000 fly balls. It's bad enough for the guy out there shagging them, but how would you like to *hit* 1,000 fly balls?"

Language, obviously, has a lot to do with some of the confusion over there. Don Blasingame, who became the first Caucasian to coach in Japan (Nankai Hawks, 1970), tells about the time he was setting his infield defense:

"I told the interpreter to tell the shortstop to move over farther into the hole," said Blasingame. "So the interpreter nods his head and runs out to the short-stop position. Now the two of them are walking around out there, and the pitcher is waiting on the mound. I mean these guys wander around for about two minutes. Then the umpire goes out to join them and he's walking around, too.

"Finally, I run out and ask, 'What in hell is going on out here? Didn't I tell you where to play?'

" 'We're looking for the hole,' said the interpreter."

Roger Repoz, who played nine years of major league baseball with the New York Yankees, Kansas City, and California, joined the Taiheyo Club Lions in 1973, then moved to the Yakult Swallows in 1974.

"The toughest place to play was Hiroshima," recalls Repoz. "The monument is there, you know, at ground zero where the atomic bomb was dropped, and it's right across from the ballpark. So every August 6 they have a festival, except that it's also an excuse for young radicals to stir up trouble. Americans were told not to go out that night, and we didn't. I remember one night I hit a home run to win a game against Hiroshima and the police had to slip me out the back door after the game. No way would they let me go out into that crowd.

"There was another home-run hitter in Japan at the same time I played, Charlie Manuel, formerly with the Minnesota Twins and a cup of coffee with the Dodgers. Charlie really had power, but those pitchers hit him right in the face. Really busted him up. Once an umpire said to Charlie, 'You're so big and strong and the pitchers are afraid of you. So I have to help them out!'

"You couldn't believe some of the umpiring over

there. It was so bad it was funny. One night we were playing in Hiroshima and about the fifth inning it started to rain. They had their ace pitcher on the mound, no score in the game, and here comes the rain. Over there, though, the fields are real sandy and usually they don't stop a game unless it's a monsoon. Well, the pitcher throws me a high fastball and I don't quite get it. It's a long fly toward the fence and the outfielder goes back with the rain in his face. You can see he's really fighting it, and the ball hits his glove, then hits the fence, then goes back into his glove. Meanwhile, I'm coming all the way around.

"Well, in Japan they use six umpires so there was a guy right out there on the play and he makes the signal: no catch, run scores!

"Well, I know what's coming. The Hiroshima manager and his entire team charge into the outfield and surround the umpire. I mean they've got the guy encircled for about 20 minutes and, sure enough, he finally runs into the middle of the field and says, 'The batter is out!'

"Now my manager walks to the top of the dugout and says, 'We will play no more.' He just stands on the top step for at least 30 minutes before he'll let us continue. It's his way of saving face, and it was the funniest thing I ever saw because everybody knew the ball hit the fence. We watched the TV replays later and just laughed."

Repoz, who broke his leg during the first season and was released (the Lions wanted to make room on their roster for Frank Howard), decided to keep a diary when he came back a year later with the Swallows, where he performed successfully through 1977.

"They couldn't pronounce my last name," said

Repoz, "so one day a team official came to me and said, 'What do you want us to call you?' I said, 'Call me Roger.' And that's exactly what they did. They put Roger on the official team roster instead of Repoz.

"I liked it there, I really did, but sometimes they did make it tough. One night I got a $200 bonus—over there they call it 'fight money'—for hitting a home run to beat the Giants. But I was lucky because the umpires favor the Giants. Everybody in Japan, it seems, wants the Giants to win.

"On this night a Japanese pitcher is throwing me fork balls in the dirt—they never threw the forkballs to Japanese hitters, just Americans—and after the umpire calls the first one in the dirt a strike, I know I've got to swing. Otherwise he's going to call me out on strikes. So I'm cursing the umpire while I'm standing there and I swing at the next one that bounces over the plate—and it's strike two. Now I foul one off and I'm still yelling at the umpire. Then the pitcher throws one that doesn't do anything. It's right down the middle and I hit it into the seats.

"I took about 15 minutes to walk around the bases."

On the night Clyde Wright left Japan he went out for a farewell dinner with his manager, Nagashima. Just the two of them, with interpreters.

"It must have cost him $500 a man," recalls Wright. "Some French joint in Tokyo with 14 courses. Then, afterward, I said 'Nagashima, is there anything I can do for you?' and he says, 'I would like to go to the Playboy Club.'

"So we get into a taxi and go to the Playboy Club, where I had a membership. He had never been there because it was voodoo for him. Somebody might think he wasn't doing his job if he was out looking at Playboy bunnies.

"So we walk into the place and everything stops. That's how surprised and honored they were to see Nagashima. The manager came over, I introduced them, and I said, 'You present Nagashima membership?' And he did. He gave him a membership. But I don't know if Nagashima ever went back."

Richie Scheinblum played in Hiroshima, but he and his wife, Mary, could never celebrate their wedding anniversary in public. They got married on August 6, the same date the bomb was dropped on Hiroshima.

"Gail Hopkins and I were the first white Americans to play for the Hiroshima Carp," said Scheinblum. "And because I'm a little silly, I think they had a hard time understanding me. I'd show up at the ballpark wearing disguises but I never knew if they appreciated it or not."

If they had a hard time with Richie, how do you think they would have felt about me? I could have made the hotfoot an international phenomenon.

The funny thing is that Americans think of baseball as *our* tradition—along with apple pie, hot dogs, and Chevrolets. I admit it's hard to think of the national pastime in the same breath with sushi and Godzilla, but you'd be amazed to see just how big the sport is in Japan.

For the record: *besuboru*, samurai style, has been in existence since 1873, when Horace Wilson, a professor at Tokyo University, first began to teach the game to the Japanese.

The first pro league was formed in 1936, two years after Babe Ruth and Lou Gehrig barnstormed in

Japan (the Bambino awed observers with 13 home runs in 18 exhibitions). By 1940 there were nine teams but because of World War II, there were no games from 1945 until 1948. By 1976 there were 12 teams, mostly owned by business firms using the teams for public relations.

To better understand what he may be getting into, any player considering a career in Japan should read *The Chrysanthemum and The Bat*, by Robert Whiting, published in 1977. I read it and that's when I realized *kojinshugi* would be my major barrier.

Whiting listed his Samurai Code of Conduct for Baseball Players in Japan—and here is a condensed version, including my comments:

1. *Players must be total team members* (no U.S. manager would argue with that concept).
2. *Players must follow established procedures* (which unfortunately, do not include players dragging infields).
3. *Players must undergo hard training* (their disabled lists are smaller; you either get into shape or else).
4. *Players must perform for the team, not individual records* (we could use a little more of that in the United States).
5. *Players must demonstrate fighting spirit* (no argument there, either).
6. *Players must behave like gentlemen on the field* (brushback pitchs and high slides are considered unethical; use of gum and tobacco is frowned upon; tempers are expected to be kept under control).
7. *Players must not be materialistic* (American owners would love this one).

8. *Players must be careful with comments to the press* (public criticism of management or team-mates is considered bad form).
9. *Players must follow the rules of sameness* (no beards, goatees, long hair, Star Patrol helmets, etc.).
10. *Players must behave like good Japanese off the field* (gambling, girls, booze are not accepted in public; good Japanese players have wives and families).
11. *Players must recognize and respect the team pecking order* (I think this means managers and coaches are allowed to slap players without getting slapped back).
12. *Players must strive for team harmony and unity* (successful teams are likened to a beautiful Japanese garden, with everything in place; emotions are to be held in check and clubhouse practical jokes are not appreciated).

As you can see, it's different. Certainly many Americans have had problems—some because of their behavior, many because they didn't perform as expected. Among those to try it, samurai style: Don Zimmer, Dick Stuart, Jim Gentile, Zoilo Versalles, Frank Howard, Don Newcombe, Jim Lefebvre, Jim Marshall, Daryl Spencer, Chico Fernandez, George Altman, Dave Roberts, Clarence Jones, John Sipin, Larry Doby, and others, all with varying results.

The first American to play in Japan was Wally Yonamine, a Hawaiian and former football player with the San Francisco 49ers, in 1951. It was just six years after the end of World War II so he was considered an Oriental Jackie Robinson.

The first time Wally slid hard into second base in

Japan he was ruled out for interference. He became a star, however (.311 lifetime), winning three Japanese batting titles.

After Yonamine, there was a Yankee stampede. Under current rules, each team is allowed to employ three foreign players, two from the major leagues and one with minor league status. And while the pay can be outstanding, most Americans earn between $100,000 and $200,000 in Japan. Also, there is taxation which once didn't exist. A 20 percent "foreign tax" comes off the top.

Unquestionably, baseball is the most popular sport in Japan. All games are televised, home and away. Yet only a few teams realize financial profit after taxes. The Sabu Lions of the Pacific League, Japanese champions in 1986, averaged 21,700 attendance for 65 home games. The Giants, who haven't won a title for three straight years, drew 2.8 million fans anyway, averaging 43,100 per game.

This, too, about American players in Japan: if we keep sending people like Randy Bass across the Pacific, certainly everybody will be happy, especially the people like Randy Bass who can demand and receive high salaries.

But for every Randy Bass there has been a Joe Pepitone.

Pepitone was perhaps the ugliest American to wear spikes in Japan. He was only 32 and possessed all of his skills when he went to Japan, yet he hardly earned his $70,000 contract. He batted just .163 for 14 games, offended many Japanese with his long hair, after-hours behavior, and crude mannerisms, and suddenly returned to the United States complaining of injuries.

One Japanese journalist was so mystified by Pepitone's actions that he suggested in print that Joe's premature baldness (yes, they discovered his toupee) was his "weak point" and caused psychological problems.

Not only did Pepi cut and run with the $70,000, he left roommate Clete Boyer with a $1,500 phone bill and a grocery bill of $1,000. After the initial outrage, the name of Pepitone became a joke in Japan. Any American player after Pepitone needed to prove himself, unless he wanted to risk the humiliation of being compared to Pepi.

Today, however, American players need to prove themselves before they can have the honor of being compared to Bass. That's another good reason why, as I approached the age of 40, I was not a good candidate to continue my baseball career in Japan.

Perhaps the era of a legitimate "World Series" between the champions of the United States and Japan is not far away. And if that day ever arrives, I'd like to be there in some capacity—maybe dragging the infield or distributing umbrella hats in the stands.

The Japanese will have no problem recognizing me. I'll be the nail sticking up that needs hammering down.

"

At USC, new players would wear an old red wig cut in a Prince Valiant hairstyle, turn their coat jackets inside out, roll up their pants legs, and parade through airports like that whenever the team would travel. The older players would make them stand on luggage carts and sing while team members threw pennies.

11
THEY DON'T TEACH THIS IN SCHOOL

On June 17, 1908, the Cincinnati Reds were in New York to play the Giants at the Polo Grounds. The game was canceled, however, to allow Yale and Princeton to use the diamond for an Ivy League championship playoff game.

College baseball had just a little more clout during the days of Teddy Roosevelt than it does today.

Yet it's now healthier (13.3 million attendance in 1986) than at any time in history.

It's also wackier.

I love college baseball even though I never played it.

Where else would you find the pitcher running into center field to shake a fielder's hand after he made a catch?

Where else would you find a group of fans (the Hammerheads, UC–Santa Barbara) attaching a bag of potato chips to a fishing rod and casting it over the fence to hang in front of a chubby enemy hitter in the on-deck circle?

I received a real taste of the college game in 1986 when I worked as analyst for ESPN and Dr. Jerry Buss's Prime Ticket Network out of Los Angeles.

Those kids can play. They're bigger, stronger, faster, and better coached today, and college baseball is fast becoming the prime feeder system for the major leagues.

Yet they are kids. The only difference today is that instead of spending four or five years in the minor leagues, talented players realize they can first go to college, then often directly into Triple-A or the major leagues. When I graduated from high school in 1963 it never entered my mind to choose college baseball over a pro contract. I just couldn't see four years of college, plus another four years in the minors before getting my shot.

But that has changed and if you don't believe it, look at Cory Snyder, Calvin Schiraldi, Pete Incaviglia, Roger Clemens, and all the others who went so quickly from campus stardom to big league stardom.

Did you know that Vice President George Bush played in the first two College World Series in 1947 and 1948? He was first baseman and captain of the Yale team that lost in the finals to USC in 1948. He wasn't a great hitter (college batting average of .250) but made only two errors in 190 chances during his senior season.

There is no evidence that first baseman Bush practiced any exorcism rituals during his college baseball days, at least, not like Ken "Voodoo" Adderley of Florida State University. Adderley, during the 1986 season, got into the batter's-box habit of flipping his bat, kissing it, then crossing himself. Apparently it worked. He broke the school's consecutive-game hitting streak record of 24.

College home run stories are my favorites. With those metal bats, it's a wonder they don't lose all their baseballs. I'm not really against kids using those clangers at the plate, but certainly the hitters have the advantage. The pitcher loses his advantage of jamming a hitter inside. How can you saw off a metal bat at the handle? You can try to jam a college hitter, and he'll take a half-swing and line one into right field. Let him try that with wood in the bigs, however, and he'll end up with splinters in his elbow. Because of their inability to jam hitters inside, you see more college pitchers perfecting the split-fingered pitch, which keeps the ball down and in the park.

Hitting a long home run, of course, doesn't always guarantee success. Mark Davis of Iona College should know. He hit one 550 feet—that's mammoth whether you're swinging ash, aluminum, or a lead pipe—against Fairfield College, only to be called out by the umpire because teammates slapped him on the back as he rounded third base.

Yes, that's interference, and instead of Davis's rocket shot over the left-field fence tying the game 12–12, Iona lost 12–11.

But, wait! There was more. Iona head coach Phil Tromdino questioned home-plate umpire Richard Citro's call vehemently (we're talking 30 minutes of vehemence), claiming that the NCAA rule book states that a team has to be warned before such a decision can be rendered. But the decision stood.

Tromdino also protested to the Metro Atlantic Athletic Conference and lost the protest. He then appealed to the NCAA Rules Committee and won, and that meant the game was actually tied, 12–12, and had to be completed from the point of the seventh-inning home run.

Iona won in the 10th on a home run by another Mark named Boshnack, and nobody came within 10 feet of him as he rounded third.

Then there was Bill Conroy's historic homer for Longwood College, Farmville, Virginia. He started from home plate in perfect form but slipped and fell on his face rounding second. The 6–4 power hitter, embarrassed, picked himself up and continued to third, where he fell headlong over the bag.

Third-base coach Buddy Bolding then took Conroy by the arm, careful not to interfere with his size 13 spikes, and escorted his prize slugger to home plate without further incident.

The umpire didn't dare call interference.

Home runs, home runs. Outfielder Greg Loyda of St. Norbert College hit one against Concordia College that went through the window of the Mequon, Wisconsin, Police Department.

But Georgia Southern's Mike Shepherd did better than that. He hit one over the center-field fence against Clemson but couldn't run because his knee-cap popped out before he could reach first base.

So now what? For 10 minutes, trainers worked on Shepherd's knee and finally carried him off the field. Georgia Southern coach Jack Stallings inserted pinch runner Frank Vashaw, who was allowed to circle the bases to complete the home run.

This one will break your heart. Middle Georgia College trailed Abraham Baldwin Agricultural College 9–7 with two outs in the bottom of the ninth inning of the Region 17 junior college tournament. Then pinch hitter Rusty Brown belted a homer over the left center-field fence with two on, and it was bedlam. Middle Georgia, the nation's number one–

ranked junior college through most of 1986, had won 10–9 to advance to the JC World Series in Grand Junction, Colorado.

Well, not exactly. It seems that Brown passed the base runner in front of him—who had stopped a few feet short of home plate to join in the celebration—and was ruled out. Middle Georgia lost 9–8, and there was no joy in Albany, Georgia. They would rather have had him strike out.

Is it always like this in college baseball or was 1986 just a wild and wacky year? Do I have any eligibility left? How about the kid from the University of Maine, Jeff Plympton, who thought his game against St. Joseph's College was scheduled for 2:30 P.M. and wandered onto the field about 1:45P.M. only to be met by a frantic coaching staff? It was a 2 o'clock game and soph Plympton—no relation to a George Plimpton of similar nonchalance—was the starting pitcher with little time for warm-up.

He threw a nine-inning no-hitter, the first for a Maine pitcher since 1950, striking out 17 and walking nobody. Another potential Wright-o?

In Jacksonville, Florida, they play for blood. Florida Junior College held intrasquad games with three teams, with the two losers required to give a pint of blood.

"We did it so their play would stay at a good level of intensity," said coach Howard Roey about his Blood Bowl. "They used to play a McDonald's Bowl where the losers bought hamburgers. I think they liked that better."

College coaches are the greatest and they're getting even better. A number of former major league stars—Tommy John and Gaylord Perry are the latest—are returning to campuses to manage.

They're joining some tough company. Some of the

giants of the past have retired—Rod Dedeaux at USC, Dick Siebert at Minnesota, Danny Litwhiler at Michigan State, Bobby Winkles at Arizona State—but certainly the top college baseball programs in the nation today are run by an elite corps.

Some of the best: Jerry Kindall (Arizona), Cliff Gustafson (Texas), Jim Brock (Arizona State), Richard "Itchy" Jones (Southern Illinois), Augie Garrido (Cal-Fullerton), Jim Dietz (San Diego State), Ron Fraser (Miami), Ron Polk (Mississippi State), Bud Middaugh (Michigan), John Winkin (Maine), Gary Ward (Oklahoma State), Gene Stephenson (Wichita State), Gary Adams (UCLA), and a pair of my West Coast favorites who assisted Dedeaux with the 1984 U.S. Olympic team, Art Mazmanian (Mt. San Antonio College) and John Scolinos (Cal Poly-Pomona).

College baseball has its humorists, too. Like Southern Illinois's Itchy Jones. A few years ago when SIU was playing in Miami, Itchy found himself in the middle of the diamond in a shouting match with an umpire.

"You missed the call!" shouted Jones.

"No," said the umpire. "Your player did not make the tag."

"My player did make the tag. He told me he made the tag."

"No," said the umpire. "He does not tell you the truth."

With that, Jones turned toward his second baseman, a youngster named Bobby Doerr.

"Then I'm going to punch my second baseman for lying to me!" he screamed at the umpire, and he began running toward the second baseman.

The astounded ump couldn't believe his eyes as Jones began shaking Doerr and yelling, "You lied to me, you lied to me."

Finally, unable to stand the sight of such injustice, the umpire ran over, grabbed Jones, and said:

"Coach, coach . . . he's not lying!"

Rod Dedeaux, who retired recently from the University of Southern California as the winningest coach in college baseball history (1,332 wins, 571 losses, 11 national titles), knew how to have fun, too. He had a tradition at USC: new players—freshmen or transfers—were forced to wear an old red wig cut in a Prince Valiant hairstyle, turn their coat jackets inside out, roll up their pants legs, and parade through airports whenever the team would travel. The older players (the salty vets, Dedeaux called them) would force the unfortunate wig wearers to stand on luggage carts, singing verses of McNamara's Band for the entire airport audience while team members threw pennies in appreciation.

Such antics were not always met with appreciation by airport security people, who more than once tried to arrest Trojan wig wearers. One young pitcher was in the process of being arrested and booked until the L.A. Police Department realized that the evidence, one red wig and a handful of pennies, had been spirited away in the confusion by an assistant coach.

Ron Fairly, ex-USC and major league first baseman, now announcer with the San Francisco Giants, tells this one on Dedeaux: USC had just won the 1958 College World Series in Omaha, Nebraska, and the Trojans were celebrating quite loudly in their hotel. Finally, tired of hearing complaints from other guests, the hotel manager went to the coach's room to investigate—only to be greeted at the door by Dedeaux himself dressed in a T-shirt and shorts. And wearing the red wig.

USC was always the target of enemy hecklers during Dedeaux's reign. When the Trojans played at

Arizona State, for example, some fan from behind the USC dugout shouted at Dedeaux: "Hey, Rod, what's it like to have seen two Halley's Comets?" And during the 1986 matchup between ASU and USC, the Trojans' portly third-base coach, Keith Brown, was surprised during the first inning when a delivery boy from Domino's Pizza showed up in the coaching box with a large pizza, courtesy of the fans behind third base.

Former USC All-America linebacker Jack Del Rio, now with the New Orleans Saints, was a catcher for the Trojans' baseball team in 1983 and 1984 and was an intimidating force on the field. Once, when USC was playing Pepperdine, tempers between the two schools flared, with the USC pitcher throwing a few high-and-tight fastballs following a Pepperdine home run.

Then, following another home run, the next Pepperdine batter was hit. That did it. The entire Pepperdine team—albeit not a very large one, physically—started to charge out of the dugout. That's when the 6'4", 235-pound Del Rio stood up, took off his mask, and took one step toward the Pepperdine team.

In unison, the Waves stopped, turned around, and returned to their dugout.

Del Rio was that intimidating. Yet when USC was playing bitter rival ASU in 1984 and another bench-emptying argument ensued, Del Rio found himself face to face with Arizona State's fiery coach, Jim Brock.

"You're going to have to hit me before you can touch anybody on my team!" shouted Brock, and there was no fight.

Brock knows how to fire up a team. Against Stan-ford in 1985—not one of ASU's memorable seasons, inasmuch as the team was on NCAA probation with six players ineligible for 20 games—Brock stalked to the mound in a game in which ASU trailed, 9–4. And, as usual, the umpire also strolled to the mound.

"Are you going to bring in another pitcher?" asked the ump.

"No," replied Brock. "We're going to fly in another fucking umpire."

Brock was kicked out of the game but the Sun Devils came back to score six runs in the bottom of the ninth to win.

And if you don't think they've had some awesome teams at Arizona State, consider the outfield of the 1984 team: in left field was Barry Bonds (Pittsburgh Pirates), the centerfielder was Oddibe McDowell (Texas Rangers), and the rightfielder was Mike Devereaux (Los Angeles Dodgers).

It may have been the greatest outfield in college baseball history, but Brock's season was hardly worry-free. On April Fool's Day 1984, for example, McDowell decided to play a joke. He got the ASU trainer to put a fake cast on his left leg. Then, limping on crutches, he walked into Brock's office and said, "Look what I did, coach."

Brock, usually full of words, was speechless. Then, finally, he said:

"There goes our national title."

"April Fool," said McDowell, my kind of guy.

So many great college players and teams have come from the West that it would be impossible to mention them all. And if you needed any proof that baseball is a sunshine sport, how about this fact: every winner of the College World Series since 1967 has come from the West or South. And that's even more reason to salute those college programs that succeed in places like Maine and Michigan.

In 1979 the Pacific-10 championship team from UCLA had six members who were still playing in the major leagues in 1986—Matt Young (Seattle, now Los Angeles), Dave Schmidt (Chicago White Sox), Pat Dodson (Boston), Tim Leary (Milwaukee, now Los Angeles), Mike Gallego (Oakland), and Don Slaught (Texas). Ironically, Jim Auten, the Pac-10 Co-Player of the Year who hit 29 home runs in 1979, had been released three years earlier by the Cubs.

It wasn't always that way at UCLA. Before Gary Adams became UCLA's head coach in 1975, a gentleman named Art Reichle coached the Bruins for 30 years. And, because crosstown rival USC was powerful, there were some lean seasons at UCLA (although Chris Chambliss led the Bruins to the College World Series in 1969). In the early seventies, in fact, things got so bad at UCLA that Reichle would let the scorekeeper draw names out of a hat to choose his starting lineup. But it still didn't help.

Craziest eligibility story of the 1986 college season: Louisburg (North Carolina) College baseball player Steve Shepard won an $18,000 automobile by sinking four shots, including a 45-footer from half court, during halftime of a basketball game.

It was one of those promotional contests during a women's game, and Shepard, a freshman pitcher, just happened to be the lucky winner.

So what?

So it's a good thing Shepard played baseball instead of basketball.

It's against NCAA rules, you see, to keep the car or money and retain eligibility. I guess the NCAA figures that if you're good enough to make a shot from half court, that makes you a pro.

So Shepard kept the car and continues to play baseball at Louisburg College. He just can't go out for the basketball team. His once-in-a-lifetime four shots made him ineligible.

Crazy things like that happen all the time on the college baseball scene. Pick up an issue of *Collegiate Baseball* and you'll find some story about a kid unable to find shoes big enough to fit him (anybody got some size 16s for pitcher Paul Steinert of Florida International University?) or a coach being charged with inciting a riot.

You may think some of those datelines are strange but, believe me, there are stranger stories. Some samples:

Napa, California—In the midst of a seven-game losing streak, Napa Valley College staged a mock funeral to bury the old team attitude, mistakes, and problems.

What happened?

Baseball items were burned behind home plate and a garlic communion followed. Napa Valley College then won three in a row, hitting .440 and scoring 15 runs.

Napa now holds a garlic communion before each game.

Houston—Can you believe six home runs in one inning? How about three of them by consecutive batters? Ever hear of a batter accomplishing a home run on a balk?

What happened?

It all started when the Rice Owls beat Southwest Texas State in a 1984 season opener, 20–0. Rice won

the other three games of the four-game series by
scores of 21–3, 19–3, and 14–0.

No, Southwest Texas did not abandon its baseball
program, but surely it was considered.

*Cookeville, Tennessee—Joe Kelley, a freshman at
Tennessee Tech, should get an award as the most
courageous performer in college baseball after getting
his first win.*

What happened?

During a 10–4 victory against Otterbein, pitcher
Kelley was hit in the eye with an elbow, requiring
stitches, and was spiked, puncturing a toenail.

Then he went inside to take a shower, accidentally
hit his mouth on the shower nozzle and chipped a
tooth.

*Sturgeon Bay, Wisconsin—It wasn't a case of draw-
ing first blood that led to a 5–5 Junior American
Legion baseball game being called in the sixth inning. It was drawing too much blood.*

What happened?

A gigantic swarm of mosquitoes descended on the
playing field, sending players, fans, and the umpire
running for shelter.

"I never saw anything like it," said Sturgeon Bay
catcher Scott Sweetman. "I must have had 20 bites
just on my legs. They were inside my mask, and I had
trouble seeing."

After 10 minutes, umpires called the game and
everybody went home to scratch.

*Fullerton, California—California State–Fullerton
coach Augie Garrido conducted a full-fledged "fu-*

neral" to bury the "negative environment" of the start of the 1985 season.

What happened?

The flag was lowered to half-mast, dirges were played over the PA system, a pyre was built over home plate, team captains served as pallbearers of an old equipment trunk filled with bats and balls, and a 1984 national championship pennant was burned and buried. New team schedules were distributed as well as new statistics sheets with all zeros.

Fullerton won its next four games.

Surely by now you've figured out that I'm a new and ardent fan of college baseball. Admittedly, I didn't pay much attention to it during my busy years trying to hit curveballs in the major leagues and wondering how to harass Ron Cey and Bill Russell. But I'm paying attention to it now and if you're looking for entertainment, I suggest that you do, too.

The College World Series, incidentally, is headed for bigger and better things—expanded eight-team, two division format with a double-elimination showdown in Omaha, Nebraska, and possible network television coverage.

That's progress. Next thing you know, they'll be asking Voodoo Adderley and Itchy Jones to sing a national anthem duet.

ONE GREAT WAY TO DEAL
WITH A TOUGH UMPIRE
1. Mention his mother.

12
JAY JOHNSTONE'S ALL-TIME GREATEST LISTS
AND OTHER ALL-TIME NONSENSE

It all started innocently enough. I was asked by *USA Today* to list my five favorite sports books, so I did:

1. Bill Lee's autobiography
2. Sparky Lyle's autobiography
3. Jimmy Piersall's *Fear Strikes Out*
4. Roger Kahn's *The Boys of Summer*
5. Naturally, my own.

So far, so good, right? No harm done, right?

Well, Lasorda didn't see it that way. We were on the road during the heat of the 1985 pennant race when *USA Today* hit the streets and he cornered me in the clubhouse.

"How come you left *my* autobiography [*The Artful Dodger*] off your list?"

"Aaaahhhh," I said, stalling, "I forgot. It was a mistake."

"Mistake! I'll tell you one thing. You better start sitting at the end of the dugout. And I'll tell you something else. Kids can read my fuckin' book. It doesn't have any bad words in it."

So I raced to the dugout phone and called *USA Today.*

"We have a problem," I told them. "I left out Tommy's book and it was an honest mistake. Could you please dump *The Boys of Summer* and put Tommy's book on top of my list, quickly?"

They never did revise the list, but they ran a little story about the flap instead. That didn't make Lasorda any happier but he didn't hold a grudge. He even allowed me to bring him some food in the locker room.

The mystery to me, though, is why people are so obsessed with lists. Mention a movie and somebody will list you his top 10. Talk about hitting and somebody will ask, "Who were the top five left-handed hitters since Ted Williams?"

OK, I'll play the game. What follows are lists, either scientifically compiled by me or stolen from someone else. Just ask Jerry Reuss.

JAY JOHNSTONE'S FIVE FAVORITE SPORTS BOOKS, REVISED

1. *The Artful Dodger* by Tom Lasorda
2. Bill Lee's *The Wrong Stuff*
3. Sparky Lyle's *The Bronx Zoo*
4. Jimmy Piersall's *Fear Strikes Out*
5. Naturally, my own. (My publisher makes me say this.)

FIVE WAYS TO KILL TIME
DURING A RAIN DELAY

If I told you all of the ways I've killed time during rain delays I'd either (a) fill a whole book or (b) get in a hell of a lot of trouble. Probably both.

1. Make collect phone calls from the dugout.
2. Think up practical jokes.
3. Play practical jokes.
4. Keep from getting caught playing practical jokes.
5. Watch it rain.

FIVE MESSIEST EX-TEAMMATES

I can't embarrass these guys by telling you *why* they're the messiest, but believe me, they're the worst. Of course, I'm the guy who shines his shoes twice a day, so I suppose you have to consider the source.

1. Bill Buckner
2. Keith Moreland
3. Larry Bowa
4. Tug McGraw
5. Ed Herrmann, Don Stanhouse (tie)

FIVE MANAGERS I MOST
ENJOYED TERRORIZING

I did not intend to overlook managers Chuck Tanner, Dick Williams, Billy Martin, Roger Craig, Bob Lemon, Bill Rigney, Rocky Bridges, Marty Marion, Bobby Wine, Sherm Lollar, or Jim Frey (well, maybe Jim Frey). I just thought the following five deserved recognition for all they've endured through their associations with me.

1. Danny Ozark
2. Lefty Phillips
3. Tom Lasorda (who is rapidly rising to the top of this list)
4. Lee Elia
5. Jim Bunning

TEN MEN I'D RATHER SEE WALK TO THE PLATE IN THE CLUTCH

1. Ted Williams
2. Mickey Mantle
3. Billy Williams
4. Pete Rose
5. Steve Garvey
6. Tony Perez
7. Mike Schmidt
8. Dale Murphy
9. Stan Musial
10. Don Mattingly

TEN WAYS TO AVOID TELEPHONE BILLS

1. Always have an excuse to use someone else's phone.
2. Call collect (say you're in a phone booth without change).
3. Use the clubhouse phone and charge your call to another person's phone number.
4. Bribe the team switchboard operator (flowers, candy, etc.).
5. Call from the manager's office.
6. Call from the general manager's office.

7. Call from the owner's office.
8. Call from your editor's office.
9. Call from the public relations office.
10. Find out the manager's credit card number.

TWENTY BEST ANSWERS TO EVERY QUESTION EVER ASKED BY SPORTSWRITERS

1. It wasn't my fault.
2. I try to give 110 percent every day.
3. Is there a gift for this interview?
4. No comment.
5. It wasn't my fault.
6. I'm not the manager.
7. We can't win them all.
8. Who's the official scorer?
9. How come you guys never come around when we're winning?
10. That information is in the press guide.
11. I was misquoted.
12. I didn't do it, Jerry Reuss did it.
13. It looks a lot easier from up there.
14. It's tough when you're not playing every day.
15. It wasn't my fault.
16. How could you call that an error?
17. It's a long season.
18. We'll be back tomorrow.
19. Don't ask me, I just work here.
20. Ask the manager. He makes out the lineup.

TWO DUMBEST QUESTIONS I'VE EVER HEARD FROM SPORTSWRITERS

1. Dick Young, *New York Post*—When interviewing Cubs pitcher Steve "Rainbow" Trout during

1984, Young asked the left-hander if he had been in communication with his father, former major league pitcher Paul "Dizzy" Trout.

The elder Trout had been dead for 12 years.

2. Ted Dawson, KABC-TV, Los Angeles—After Mike Witt beat the Boston Red Sox in Game One of the 1986 American League playoffs, Dawson shouted in a press conference to Angels manager Gene Mauch, "Was this the best game you've ever seen Witt pitch?"

"No," said Mauch. "I saw him pitch a perfect game in 1984."

THREE DUMBEST ANSWERS I'VE EVER HEARD FROM ATHLETES

1. Henry Tillman, Olympic boxing gold medalist, when asked how far his boyhood home in Los Angeles was from the Coliseum, site of the boxing finals:

"Oh, about three or four miles, depending on the traffic."

2. George Rogers, Washington Redskins running back, when asked if he had any personal goals:

"1,500 or 2,000 yards, whichever comes first."

3. Ex-Dodger Reggie Smith, when asked to assess an important playoff series:

"I just hope the best team is able to submerge."

JAY JOHNSTONE'S FAVORITE BASEBALL TRIVIA QUESTION

There have been nine players in the history of baseball to win back-to-back Most Valuable Player Awards and they just happen to fill all nine positions on the playing field. Who were they and what were their positions?

JAY JOHNSTONE'S FAVORITE BASEBALL TRIVIA ANSWER

C—Yogi Berra, Yankees (1954–55)
P—Hal Newhouser, Tigers (1944–45)
1B—Jimmy Foxx, Philadelphia A's (1932–33)
2B—Joe Morgan, Reds (1975–76)
3B—Mike Schmidt, Philadelphia Phillies (1980–81)
SS—Ernie Banks, Cubs (1958–59)
OF—Dale Murphy, Braves (1982–83)
OF—Mickey Mantle, Yankees (1956–57)
OF—Roger Maris, Yankees (1960–61)

SIX WAYS TO BREAK IN A ROOKIE

1. Convince him to appear in uniform for a taping of "Good Morning America" at 8 A.M. on a Sunday morning during spring training when practice begins at noon. They fall for this every time.
2. Ask him to submit a sperm sample to the team nurse.
3. Nail his shoes to the floor.
4. The oldie-but-goodie hotfoot in the dugout.
5. After he's had a bad game, have his bag packed in front of his locker with the attached note: "See the Manager."
6. Charge room service bills to his hotel room on first road trip.

BEST WAY TO BREAK IN A NEW BATBOY

1. Send him to the bullpen to bring back the key to the batter's box.

FIVE SLOPPIEST TOBACCO CHEWERS

1. Lefty Phillips (the only man I ever knew who was rejected by every laundry in town).
2. Yogi Berra (he can spray you from any angle).
3. Bill Buckner (he gets more around his mouth than inside it).
4. Rocky Bridges (he gets it all over everything).
5. John Vukovich (guard your coffee at all times).

MY FIFTEEN FAVORITE FLAKES

1. Curt Blefary (he owns the Cuckoo Lounge in Florida, so what does that tell you?).
2. Tug McGraw (a premeditated joker; he'd plan for weeks).
3. Sparky Lyle (onetime caretaker of the Bronx Zoo).
4. Dick-Dirt Tidrow (the last time he was clean they spanked and burped him).
5. Bill Lee (truly baseball's Spaceman).
6. Al Hrabosky (but now he's shaven and trying to go straight).
7. Jim Piersall (he was my first roomie and the reason I'm the way I am today).
8. Mickey Hatcher (anyone who puts a pig in Tom Lasorda's office makes my list).
9. John Lowenstein (claims he smashed cakes to save lives).
10. Kurt Bevacqua (he can make Lasorda sputter by just looking at him).
11. Randy Jones (don't let that Little Orphan Annie face fool you).
12. Joe Azcue (owns the Catcher's Mitt Lounge in Kansas City).
13. Greg Minton (anybody named "Moon Man" deserves a place on this list).

14. Doug Rader (he could sit on birthday cakes with the best of them).
15. Yours truly (just in case this ends up in a time capsule).

FIVE BEST BALLPARK SHOWERS IN THE NATIONAL LEAGUE

1. Cincinnati
2. Houston
3. Los Angeles
4. San Diego
5. Philadelphia

FIVE WORST SHOWERS IN THE NATIONAL LEAGUE

1 and 2. Atlanta and Chicago (tie)
3. Montreal
4. St. Louis
5. Chicago jail

FIVE TOUGHEST UMPIRES I EVER DEALT WITH

1. Ed Runge
2. Ed Runge
3. Ed Runge
4. Ed Runge
5. Paul Runge (his son)

ONE GREAT WAY TO DEAL WITH A TOUGH UMPIRE

1. Mention his mother.

RICHIE SCHEINBLUM'S LIST OF THE FIVE GREATEST MEN WHO EVER LIVED

1. Jesus Christ
2. Albert Einstein
3. Sigmund Freud
4. Karl Marx
5. Sandy Koufax

FIVE MOST VICIOUS QUOTES ABOUT THE BELOVED CHICAGO CUBS

1. "Will the lady who left her nine children at Wrigley Field please come and get them? They're beating the Cubs, 13–0, in the 7th."— Chicago radio announcer
2. "Cub Fever! Catch It and Die."—T-shirt at Wrigley Field
3. "The only bad thing about being released by the Cubs is they made me keep my season tickets."— Ken Reitz
4. "The World's Greatest Newspaper now owns the World's Worst Baseball Team."—*Sports Illustrated*
5. "The Cubs were taking batting practice and the pitching machine threw a no-hitter."—Chicago morning disc jockey

JAY JOHNSTONE'S TWENTY-FIVE FAVORITE CLASSIC COLEMANISMS

These are on-the-air utterances from the mouth of San Diego Padres announcer Jerry Coleman. I tried to cut this list to 10, but it was just impossible.

Sometimes I try to imagine Coleman chatting with Yogi Berra, but it's too bizarre to even think about.

1. "Hector Torres, how can you communicate with Enzo when he speaks Spanish and you speak Mexican?"
2. "The batter has no balls."
3. "Dawson got to the ball about the time the ball did."
4. "Well, it looks like the All-Star balloting is about over, especially in the National and American Leagues."
5. "The first pitch to Tucker Ashford is grounded into left field. No, wait a minute. It's ball one, low and outside."
6. "We're all sad to see Glenn Beckert leave. Before he goes, though, I hope he stops by so we can kiss him goodbye. He's that kind of guy."
7. "Rich Folkers is throwing up in the bullpen."
8. "Nate Colbert swings and misses and it's fouled back."
9. "Swung on and fouled back for strike three."
10. "Hendrick simply lost that sun-blown pop-up."
11. "Cleveland and Toronto are playing in the ninth and that's a final."
12. "After five full innings, we're still where we started the day, Padres 2, Phillies 2."
13. "They throw Winfield out at second base but he's safe."
14. "Whenever you get an inflamed tendon, you've got problems. OK, here's the next pitch to Gene Tendon."
15. "It's snowing in Detroit. Boy, that wind really

plays havoc with a game when it blows in off Lake Michigan. (pause) What? (pause) Well, I was only three lakes away."

16. "If Rose's streak was still intact, with that single to left, the fans would be throwing babies out of the upper deck."

17. "From the way Denny's shaking his head, he's either got an injured shoulder or a gnat in his eye."

18. "Senior Citizens' Day is Sunday. And if you want to become a senior citizen, just call the Padre office."

19. "The Phillies are flexing their fangs out there now."

20. "Next up is Fernando Gonzalez, who is not playing tonight."

21. "The shoe is starting to move to the other foot."

22. "That bunt was perfect except that it went foul."

23. "Ozzie Smith just made another play that I've never seen anyone else make before, and I've seen him make it more than anyone else ever has."

24. "Getting hit on the fingers with a pitch is a great way to break them. There are a lot of broken fingers running around that way."

25. "A day without newspapers is like walking around without your pants on."

AND JUST TO SHOW THAT JERRY COLEMAN ISN'T THE ONLY ONE . . .

1. "Last time up he struck out and flied to center."—Dodger announcer Vin Scully

2. "The pitcher is hitting in the on-deck circle."— Padres announcer Dave Campbell
3. "He's been a former outfielder most of his career."—Dodger announcer Ross Porter
4. "The Angels are holding on to a 2–1 deficit."— Angels announcer Bob Starr
5. "Now that I see the replay, that most definitely could have been."—Lakers announcer Keith Erickson
6. "The players who didn't make the trip from Vero remained in Vero."—Dodgers announcer Jerry Doggett
7. "The California Angels required Tommy John from the New York Yankees."—Ex-L.A. radio announcer Tommy Hawkins
8. "It could permanently hurt a batter for a long time."—Pete Rose, on the brushback pitch
9. "Today in other Olympic hockey games, West Germany plays Yugoslavia and the USSR takes on Portland . . . ahhh, that should read Poland."—Hawkins

FIVE MEN I'D PREFER TO SPEND TIME WITH ON THE DISABLED LIST

1. Jerry Reuss—My greatest great partner.
2. Don Stanhouse—He *earned* his nickname "Stan the Man Unusual."
3. Tug McGraw—His covert clubhouse maneuvers were a great inspiration to me.
4. Steve Garvey—Hanging around with The Garv helps your image.
5. Tom Lasorda—The best in the history of baseball at getting free meals.

ELEVEN LONGEST HOME RUNS I'VE PERSONALLY WITNESSED

1 and 2. Harmon Killebrew—Two, both in the old Minnesota ballpark: one off Jack Sanford of the Angels into the upper deck, the other a line drive off the upper deck facade one day later, off Lew Burdette
3. Frank Howard—Upper deck, RFK Stadium, Washington, D.C.
4. Reggie Jackson—All-Star Game, Tiger Stadium, Detroit
5. Tom Egan—*Over* the roof, Comiskey Park, Chicago
6. Mickey Mantle—Upper deck, Yankee Stadium, New York
7. Willie Stargell—Upper deck, Veterans Stadium, Philadelphia
8. Greg Luzinski—Off the bell in center field, Veterans Stadium
9. Dick Allen—Center-field bleachers, Comiskey Park
10. Dave Kingman—Down the street, six houses away, Wrigley Field, Chicago
11. Jay Johnstone—Moon shot off Pat Zachary, upper deck, Veterans Stadium. And there's still a seat painted for me there. Bob Uecker sits in it when he goes to Phillies games.

BEST SALOONS AROUND THE NATIONAL LEAGUE

Now, as everyone knows, ballplayers never hang out in saloons. So I've called on a national expert, my dear friend and cowriter Rick Talley, to help me with this list. So, based on anonymous contributions from the Los Angeles chapter of the Baseball Writers Association of America, Mr. Talley and friends offer this Guide to Being Overserved from Coast to Coast.

SAN DIEGO

Kelly's Piano Bar at the Town and Country Hotel— Loud piano player, thick carpeting in case of accidental fall, friendly bartender, honest 2 A.M. closing, cocktail waitresses with cleavage.

SAN FRANCISCO

Silhouette's—A dark disco off Washington Square with oldies music and women of all shapes and sizes.

Lefty O'Doul's—Anchor Steam beer, piano bar, decent Irish coffee, but a tough bar for heavy drinking because the steps to the men's room are steep and it makes for a shaky climb back. The stagger back to the team hotel, however, is also downhill, so that's a plus.

Capp's Corner—Friendly proprietor with cigar and derby hat. One umpire we know of once spent $300 there in a single evening.

Bobby Mulherne's—On Buchanan in the Marina district. A little fancy for some writers' tastes, but they pour generous portions of straight vodka and sometimes the owner buys.

HOUSTON

Kay's Lounge—Pearl Beer with dust on the bottles (the bartender says the locals won't drink the stuff); loud country & western music, including

Red Steagall singing "Lone Star Beer and Bob Wills' Music" on the jukebox; and a table in the shape of Texas (which makes for easier drinking than one in the shape of, say, Delaware).

CINCINNATI

Walt's Hitching Post—Operated by a Bill Melton, not the ex-player, who likes horses. The ribs are excellent and occasionally you can find National League umpires racing barefoot in the parking lot.

Island's—Located on the Mississippi River but no writers have drowned there. Yet.

ATLANTA

Fitzgerald's—Cocktails are served in milkshake glasses, so what else do you need to know?

PHILADELPHIA

Saloon Restaurant—A drink that's a drink and lots of great sports memorabilia.

ST. LOUIS

Missouri Bar & Grill—Werewolf Mort once chased a shot of Jack Daniels with a shot of tabasco here. The joint was made famous by Rick Hummel of the local *Post-Dispatch* (so famous it was shut down for three days for violating closing hours). Great pinball machines, late-night food, noise, and newspaper printers drinking Busch Bavarian from the bottle.

Gitto's Pasta House—Great pasta, friendly waitresses, and a perfect place for lunch.

CHICAGO

Hangge-Uppe—4 A.M. closing, whiskey on two levels, great sports trivia machines, variety of shooters, dance floor to avoid.

(Editor's Note: The panel disagreed violently on further Chicago listings but gave blanket approval of any other saloons within five-mile radius of State and Division streets.)

PITTSBURGH

Costanzo's—Sleeper of the National League, frequented by baseball traditionalists Headgear and Tierack, women's bowling teams, and other customers of questionable background.

NEW YORK

Runyon's—At 50th and 3rd, named after a fellow named Damon. Friendly host Joe Healy, but too much talk about the Giants, the Yankees, and Villanova.

MONTREAL

Aulte Munich Beer Garten—Order pitchers of beer with no glasses, dance with strangers, and learn to speak French.

Hunter's Horn—Bilingual women, but difficult trivia machine because of so many hockey questions.

LOS ANGELES

Nikola's—Near Dodger Stadium, run by grumpy Yugoslavs. Large TV screen, low prices, good food.

Shortstop—Across the street from Nikola's, a cop hangout with hot popcorn, pool tables.

Pacific Dining Car—In downtown L.A., too nice and expensive for writers but recommended for those with more class.

And finally, this list from my friend Daryl Brilliant and his friend Andy Carbone. I'm still trying to figure out what criteria they used to compile this All-Classic Team, but I'm just relieved to have made the list. I think.

DARYL BRILLIANT AND ANDY CARBONE'S ALL-CLASSIC TEAM

Starting Team
P—Ross Baumgarten
C—George Mitterwald
1B—Larry Biittner
2B—Sandy Alomar
3B—Butch Hobson
SS—Don Kessinger
RF—Rusty Staub
CF—Tom Grieve
LF—Mike Jorgensen

Second Team
P—Wilbur Wood
C—Jerry Grote
1B—Mike Lum
2B—Mike Tyson
3B—Tim Foli
SS—Mark Belanger
RF—Manny Mota
CF—Jay Johnstone
    (every team needs a
    personality)
LF—Tommy Davis

Honorable Mention: Pete Broberg, Tom House, Jim Barr, Dick Pole, Fred Norman, Matt Alexander, Joe Ferguson, Bob Bailey, Pat Putnam, Gary Thomasson, Roger Metzger, Rick Monday, Reggie Smith, Claude Osteen, Ed Armbrister, Bill Plummer, Cesar Geronimo, Champ Summers, Steve Braun, Mario Mendoza, Bill Stein, Barry Foote, Manny Sanguillen, Pat Kelly, Dave Skaggs, Sam Mejias, Rennie Stennett, Ted Sizemore, and Don Stanhouse.

Poor ol' Luke Appling, 80 years old, tripped over his shoes in Atlanta, got a leg cramp, and couldn't get up. It was funny, but not funny. Maybe the best way to hold an Old-Timers Game is to let everybody walk to the first baseline, wave to the audience, then go have a banquet.

13
AT LEAST I CAN STILL STAND UP

I'm not sure whether the fellow who invented Old-Timers Games should be the target of coronation or castration.

Maybe that's because I'm just learning to be an Old-Timer, i.e., one who played professional baseball but now only talks about it.

Age, incidentally, has nothing to do with being an Old-Timer. It's a state of mind. As Duane Kuiper, former major league infielder, said when playing his first Old-Timers game at age 35, "It's not how old you are, it's how old you feel. And I feel as old as any of those guys."

Me, too, fella. I celebrated my 40th birthday last November and I played in my first Old-Timers Games last summer. I was a star. I'm playing in Cincinnati in September when one of those old farts tosses one right down the gut on 0 and 2 and the umpire starts to call me out, then pulls back his hand and says: "Oh,

189

I almost forgot. I'm not supposed to call anybody out."

"Hey, what's going on around here?" yells the catcher, old Johnny Bench, but I sort of liked it. Where were umpires like that when I was an active player?

It was the first summer for the Equitable Old-Timers Baseball Series during 1986 and it was a success. There were 26 games in 26 parks and, although I didn't make it to all of them, I got a full taste. The money raised went into a fund for older ballplayers not sufficiently covered by the current ballplayers' pension fund, and I think that's a great idea. We raised $260,000 last summer, and Ralph Branca is president of the organization that administers the fund. Vice-presidents are Joe Garagiola, Rusty Staub, and Bob Gibson.

Nostalgia is what makes Old-Timers Games. I had a loyal baseball fan tell me that one of his greatest thrills was seeing Billy Williams hit a grand slam off Hoyt Wilhelm at Comiskey Park during the Old-Timers Game connected with the 50th anniversary All-Star Game in 1983. I can understand that. Hoyt still tilts his head to one side and the knuckleball can't travel much slower now than it ever did. And Billy, the sweet swinger from Whistler, Alabama, didn't make it to Cooperstown by accident. He's a deserving new member of the Hall of Fame.

I went from part-time Dodger in 1985 to full-time Old-Timer in 1986 with no adjustment problems, mainly because an injured hip didn't allow me much opportunity to play in '85, anyhow. I probably gained three pounds between careers and that was it. Otherwise, I'm as active as when I was a player—running, doing aerobics, giving my daughter a hotfoot—everything but staying up half the night waiting for games to end.

My main frustration is not sticking with the more stringent regular exercise. I tried, but it just doesn't work and I figure that if I gain three pounds a year for the next 20 years I might have a problem. You do see some fatties at the Old-Timers Games. I took one look at Ernie Banks, remembered how slim and slender he once was, and said to myself, "Uh-oh, it may not be as easy as you think." On the other hand, he can still hit a fastball, so maybe there's hope for me.

The thing we aching Old-Timers have to worry about, too, is getting hurt. My pal Tom Egan swung at a Bob Gibson slider last summer and threw out his back. Richie Scheinblum started to run to first base and his arthritis got him. Everybody in the dugout was moaning, groaning, and laughing at the same time.

Poor ol' Luke Appling, 80 years old on April 2, 1987, tripped over his shoes in Atlanta, got a leg cramp, and couldn't get up. It was funny, but not funny. Albie Pearson pulled a leg muscle diving for a line drive, which he missed. These guys remember all the remarkable things they could do, but now some of them can't do anything. Maybe the best way to hold an Old-Timers Game is to let everybody walk to the first baseline, wave to the audience, then go take a seat.

Already I'm saying to myself, "How am I going to look? How will I feel?" When you're a ballplayer you never expect to get old. Your knees should always be flexible, your legs strong. But I guess it doesn't work that way.

In addition to the Equitable games, I got Old-

Timers invitations last summer from some of my former clubs—the Angels, Padres, Phillies, and Cubs. I didn't hear from the White Sox, though. Maybe that summer of '72 in Chicago when I hit .188 disqualified me. Or maybe Sox owner Eddie Einhorn remembered that I once roomed with Jimmy Piersall.

One thing I wasn't so crazy about was attending all those Old-Timers banquets. Whew, there's a lot of lying going on at those things. I'm sitting there one night listening to the speeches and asking myself, "I gotta listen to this for the next 20 years?"

Old-Timers are worse than old fishermen.

Yet the memories do make it worthwhile. I had almost forgotten about Bill Melton breaking his nose on a pop fly. Rich Morales reminded me at one of the Old-Timers Games, and even Melton had to laugh at the retelling. The Sox were in Baltimore in 1972 (yes, the year I hit .188), and third baseman Melton drifted over near the dugout to catch the pop-up. At the last moment, though, he started worrying about the dugout steps and took one quick glance. That's when the ball hit him in the nose.

Appling told me a story, too (after we helped him up and back into the dugout): It was early one season, chilly but clear, and wives of some of the players were seated down the right-field line where they could catch the sun. Included in the group of about a half-dozen was Appling's wife, only he didn't know it.

If you're any kind of baseball fan, young or old, you know that Luke Appling could hit more foul balls than any player in history. Anyhow, on this day he lined about six or seven foul rocket shots into the section where the wives were seated. Finally, his wife turned in anger to the others and said, "I'm sorry, ladies, but we'd all better get out of here. Luke and I had an argument this morning and I know he's trying to hit me."

"I didn't even know she was there," said Appling. "Honest."

He did relish telling about the time his cheap bosses at the White Sox wouldn't provide baseballs for him to give away at public appearances. Luke had made about 15 or 20 speaking appearances, representing the Sox, and he wasn't even getting paid.

"I even had to pay my own cab fares," he recalled. "Then I started running out of baseballs to give away, so I asked for another dozen."

He was told, however, that the team didn't have another dozen to spare. "Go down to the sporting goods store and buy them yourself," they said.

"Oh, is that so?" said Appling. "I think I've got a better way." Luke posted a couple of his buddies in a certain section of the ballpark and proceeded to hit 11 in a row to them during batting practice.

"I didn't quite get my dozen," said Luke. "I got tired."

The neat thing about being a fledgling Old-Timer is swapping stories with the veteran Old-Timers. Like Bill "Moose" Skowron. Now there was a man: lifetime batting average of .282, 211 home runs, eight World Series appearances with those great New York Yankee teams of the mid-fifties and early sixties, and a great crew-cut.

Moose is only 56 and still strong enough to jack a fastball out of any park in America. The thing I admire about him, though, is how he talks about his manager, the late Casey Stengel:

"It was my first year [1954] in the major leagues," said Moose, during one of the Old-Timers game's time-outs, "and Casey had me hitting cleanup. Bases were loaded, nobody out, bottom of the first inning in Yankee Stadium, 61,000 people yelling like crazy and what does he do? He calls me back into the dugout. I couldn't believe it. I was so mad I threw the bat and hit him in the leg. Eddie Robinson pinch hit, doubled, and we went ahead, 3–0. I was so angry that I left the ballpark, went back to the hotel, and listened to the rest of the game, which we won, on the radio.

"Now it's the next day and when I arrive at the park, Casey calls me into his office. He closes the door and says, 'Moose, don't you ever show me up again. I don't care how you feel but I'm out there to win.'

" 'But Case,' I said 'I love to hit. Bases loaded, nobody out, first inning, how can you take me out?'

" 'That's my prerogative,' he said, and that was it.

"But I never forgot that conversation. I never challenged him again.

"Then, two years later, in the 1956 World Series, it was almost the same situation: bases loaded, nobody out, and I was 0 for 8 in the Series. And as I'm headed for home plate I hear this whistle and I'm saying to myself, 'Oh, no, not again.' I walk over to Stengel in the dugout and he says, 'Moose, there are no outs.'

" 'I know, Case. And I know Roger Craig is pitching.'

" 'Then I want you to take two shots to right field.'

" 'OK, OK.'

"Now I walk to the plate and Roy Campanella is grinning at me. 'See, Moose,' Campy says in that squeaky voice, 'I knew ol' Case would let you hit.'

"Well, I hit a grand-slam homer on the first pitch— pulled it dead into the left-field seats. It was my only hit of the Series. And as I come back into the dugout,

Stengel is waiting and says, 'Moose, that's the way to hit the ball to left field.'

"I'll never forget that man. God, how I respected him."

Those were the days, however, when ballplayers had little or no leverage in negotiations. Skowron hit .319, .308, and .304 from 1955 through 1957, all pennant-winning years for the Yankees, and never got a pay raise. They kept telling him about all the good players behind him in the minor leagues and Moose kept signing the contracts.

"They even tried to cut my pay $5,000 after we lost the 1957 Series to Milwaukee," said Moose. "They benched me in that Series and used Harry "Suitcase" Simpson, instead, and he went 1 for 12 and we lost. Then they said, 'Moose, we lost the Series, so you have to take a $5,000 cut.'

" 'Hey,' I said, 'can I help it if Harry Simpson went 1 for 12?' "

Stengel seems to pop up frequently in conversation when Old-Timers get together to old-time. So much so, in fact, that I'm convinced I should have been an Original Met under Casey. That must have been some fun. Over there I would have been just another one of the guys. Phils announcer Richie Ashburn, who finished his illustrious 15-year playing career with Casey's Mets in 1962, tells this story about Stengel and the remarkable base-running abilities of Marvelous Marv (he had the name before Hagler) Throneberry.

Throneberry is batting late in the game with the bases loaded and the Mets trailing by a couple of runs. He triples, everybody scores, and it looks as if the Mets have won.

There was only one problem. Actually, two. Everybody in the dugout noticed that Marv had missed first base. The Cubs also saw it, flipped the ball to Ernie Banks, and Throneberry was called out for the third out. The runs don't count and Casey jumps out of the dugout and starts screaming at the first-base umpire. It's a helluva' argument, one of those nose-to-nose matches, and Stengel is doing just fine until the second-base umpire walks over, taps him on the shoulder, and says "Casey, I hate to tell you this, but he also missed second base."

Stengel, for just a split second, was silent. Then he said: "Well, I know damned well he didn't miss third. He's standing on it!"

One theme that remains constant when Old-Timers get together, either in uniform or in a saloon, is that "something is missing" from today's game. Perhaps it's always been that way, from one generation to the next, that things were never like the "good old days." Ex-ballplayers do have a point because many of them are still around the game as coaches or broadcasters and they *see* the difference.

Stan Williams, who pitched 14 seasons in the big leagues (109–94) and now scouts for the Yankees, sings the familiar lament, "There just isn't the camaraderie we had," says Williams. "We had to pool money for a beer in those days [he was a rookie with the Dodgers in 1958]. When the Dodgers went on the road you could expect the entire pitching staff to be lined up at the bar that night, including the catcher, Johnny Roseboro. The only guy who would be missing would be the next day's starting pitcher and even he would come in for a couple and then leave. That's just the way it was. We hung together.

"When I was with the Indians, we had this one bar in Milwaukee which was redecorated four years in a row. It started out as just a dive, but each year we'd come back it would be redesigned or have new chairs. Finally, it got so nice we didn't want to drink there anymore."

Williams is convinced that most baseball players are pyromaniacs, and I can't argue with him. Give a ballplayer a book of matches in the dugout or clubhouse and you can get ready to send for the fire brigade.

"Once in Cleveland I was taking a five-inning nap," recalled Williams, "and this big pitcher, Gary Kroll, decides he's gonna' have some fun with me. Now, understand, I was 6'5" and weighed 230, but Kroll stood at least an inch taller. He was built like Adonis and was one of those running freaks—you know, go out and run 20 miles in the morning, then do push-ups in front of you. That guy could really run. He couldn't get anybody out but he could run. Anyhow, I'm back in the clubhouse sleeping—no big deal, I always got up about the fifth inning in case they needed me—and Kroll lit my shoestrings on fire.

"The only thing that really made me mad was that he was such a cheap son of a bitch. I mean really cheap. He wouldn't spend a quarter for anything. So after he lights up my shoestrings I have to get the clubhouse boy to run for my other shoes while I'm inspecting my toes for damage. Then I go into the game and finish. Now he comes into the clubhouse and I say, 'OK, Gary, you've had your free one. That's all you get.'

"Well, he couldn't stand it. Two weeks later he lit me again, burned my feet and everything. Then one day I work two innings, leave for a pinch hitter, and go into the clubhouse alone. Well, you know what's coming. I head straight for his locker, take his new

$90 street shoes, and stuff them with paper. Then I squirt lighter fluid into them and wait for him to come through the door.

"Well, the game ends, here comes Kroll, and I light the match. You talk about some son of a bitch wanting to cry. That guy was dying. But what was he going to do? It was payback, that's all."

Baseball players look up to certain other players. It's natural. You don't want to admit it but there are men who simply command your respect. Like I've always looked to Ted Williams as some kind of god. And I've heard pitchers talk about Sandy Koufax like he belonged on another planet.

Stan Williams looked up to Frank Howard. He thought he was Superman. "We even called him Superman," said Williams. "We played some winter ball together and people had never seen anything like him. He would hit balls so far, just out of sight, that the other guys felt like little kids.

"And if you ever saw Frank eat, oh, my God! You think he's big now? Well, he was big enough then, too [6'7", 265 pounds]. He could eat seven meals while you ate one. When he went into a restaurant other people would just put down their forks to watch him eat. They were in awe. And he'd have his little wife, Carol, with him. She must have weighed 103 pounds, and when he finished his seven meals, he'd pick up what was left of Carol's meal and scrape it off onto his plate.

"Well, people idolized Frank Howard and I can understand why. What a fine man he was and remains today [Howard coaches with Seattle].

"Eddie Roebuck and I were crazy, though. We'd tell

taxi drivers that Frank was queer. Pretty weird sense of humor, huh? Those cabbies would get the damnedest expressions on their faces. They just couldn't believe that this giant was queer—which he wasn't, of course. Geez, if Frank had ever found out, he'd have pinched our heads off."

Remember Dick Groat? What a winner he was over 14 major league seasons, twice playing on teams that won the World Series in seventh games—the Pirates in 1960 and the Cardinals in 1964.

Groat remembers an incident from that 1964 Series with considerable glee. Like I said, there are some things a player never forgets:

"We were in Yankee Stadium," said Groat, "and the Series was tied at one game apiece. Now the score is tied, bottom of the ninth, and our great closer at the time, Barney Schultz, comes in from the bullpen. Barney, though, threw a knuckleball that didn't knuckle and Mickey Mantle, a notorious low-ball hitter, hit a rocket home run which reached the third deck in about five seconds. When he hit it I just ran over to third base where Ken Boyer stood. I knew the game was over. Well, Mike Shannon was playing right field for us that season and Mike's a little goofy anyhow, so while the ball was drilling a hole into the upper deck seats, Shannon jumps on the right-field railing and acts like he's going to make the catch. Well, even though we lost and were down a game in the Series, it was really a funny sight.

"Now it's Game Four, also in Yankee Stadium, and we're behind 3–0 in the first inning. Mantle is the base runner on second base and we're changing pitchers. Roger Craig has come into the game for us and while he's warming up, I'm standing on second chatting with Mickey, telling him about the stunt Shannon pulled the day before.

"Roger had a magnificent pickoff to second base, but I had Mantle so engrossed in my story that he wasn't even paying attention to him when play resumed. Then, just as I was getting to the punch line, Mickey turns his head to look at the spot where Shannon had jumped onto the railing.

"That's when Craig whirled and made the pickoff throw. Mickey was a dead duck and it was the only time in his career he was ever picked off second base. Craig and Ron Taylor went on to shut out the Yankees the rest of the way, Ken Boyer hit a grand slam, and we won, 4–3. And, as you know, we also won the Series in seven games.

"Mantle, to this day, keeps reminding me about the day I told him a story while picking him off second base in front of a national TV audience in the World Series."

There are certain incidents that never leave a baseball player's mind. Old-Timers, in fact, can remember the location of every pitch and what the fan behind home plate was shouting. And if they can't remember, they'll make it up. There was nothing fictitious, though, about Stan Williams's memory of batting against Sal "The Barber" Maglie:

"I was a slow worker when I first came up in 1958," said Stan, "and I guess it agitated some of the players on other teams. So in this game at the Coliseum in L.A., I'm pitching against the Cardinals, top of the fourth inning, and I'm really struggling. They've got a couple of runners on base and it must have taken me 20 minutes to get out of the inning. And it was one of those really hot smoggy days, too.

"Finally, I get out of the inning but barely get into the dugout before our first two hitters are retired by Maglie. Now I'm the hitter and I'm still exhausted, so I'm fiddling with my jacket, walking slowly, anything to kill time.

"This does not make Sal happy. This is his last major league season and he's been through a lot of battles and wars on that pitching mound. He does not need this rookie stalling with him in the hot sun.

"Finally, I step into the batter's box and he throws me two hellacious curve balls—strike one, strike two—I've got no chance. So now it's 0 and 2 and he decides he'll get cute. He calls time-out, sits down on the mound, takes off one shoe, dumps the dirt out of it, then does the same with the other. The fans are roaring because they know he's making fun of me. I do not think it's funny.

"So now he's up again, gets the sign, and I just know it's another curveball. But just before he pitches, I step out of the box. I'm thinking, 'Screw this guy ... I'm not going to let him show me up.' The only problem is that Maglie didn't earn that 'Barber' nickname by singing Figaro. He'd shave your chin with a fastball without hesitation. But, hey, I knew I couldn't hit his curve so I'm hoping to lure him into a fastball.

"Well, he's not smiling anymore. There's a scowl on his face, in fact, and I figure he's coming right at me, which he did—he smokes me right under the chin, but I open up and jerk the ball about 450 feet into the left-field stands for a home run, my very first in the major leagues. Man, I ran around those bases as fast as I could."

And that's how it goes at Old-Timers Games. The men who played in the thirties, forties, fifties, and sixties—and now us oldies-but-goodies who also played in the seventies and eighties—gather each summer for our own hit-and-giggle brand of baseball and, best of all, story-telling.

One day, when he's finished dazzling them in Texas, Charlie Hough will reminisce about the night he lost a no-hitter in Anaheim Stadium, then forgot to cover home plate and also lost the game. Dave Henderson will recount every pitch before hitting that home run off Donnie Moore in the 1986 AL playoff, and what kind of stories do you think Len Dykstra will have to tell?

Maybe, by then, Bill Buckner can chuckle with Leon Durham about missed ground balls and Mike Scott can tell everybody how he *really* threw that pitch.

As for me, well, I was just a rookie Old-Timer last summer. I'm just getting warmed up. I've still got lots of time to make up some great stories.

Bill Madlock dressed a 400-pound fan in Mike Scioscia's uniform shirt and put him in the cage for batting practice.

Reggie Jackson got so upset one night in Cleveland he broke every light bulb in the tunnel leading from the dugout to the clubhouse. The rest of the Yankees stumbled back in darkness.

When retired and overweight Willie Stargell went to Atlanta to coach, someone suggested they get a couple of drive-in movie screens to make him some uniform pants.

And I'm over the edge?

14
I'M OVER
THE EDGE?

A couple of months ago I went into Richie Scheinblum's jewelry showroom in Anaheim, rattled the
security door, and shouted, "It's a holdup!" Richie's
customers flattened against the wall and the saleswo-
man ran for the alarm button.

"Hey, Jay," said Richie, "long time, no see."

The next time I tried a different tactic. I grabbed
my chest, started gasping, did a full 360, and fell flat
to the floor.

"Heart attack!" yelled somebody. "Call the
paramedics!"

"No, caffeine attack," I said, jumping up. "Got any
coffee, Richie?"

Which reminds me of my favorite coffee story:

The airline pilot picks up the cockpit microphone
after takeoff and says to the baseball team aboard as
passengers, "Welcome aboard, fellows. We'll be cruis-
ing about 30,000 feet and we should have a smooth

trip with little turbulence. We're right on time and should land in Chicago about 4 o'clock local time, so sit back, enjoy the trip, and best of luck against the Cubs."

He then turns to his copilot, but forgets to turn off the microphone.

"All I need now to make this a perfect day," said the pilot, "would be a hot cup of coffee and that blond stewardess."

Well, you can imagine the reaction in the main cabin, where everyone heard the pilot's comments being broadcast. The stewardess in the back of the plane also heard them and began running up the aisle to warn the pilot to turn off the mike switch before saying anything else.

But before she could reach the cockpit, one of the passengers shouted:

"Hey, honey . . . don't forget the coffee."

Nothing is sacred to chauvinist pig baseball players.

Remember reading about the "Horse's Balls of Chicago" in *Temporary Insanity*? If you didn't read it, a quick review: at the corner of Belmont Avenue and Sheridan Road in Chicago stands a statue of General Philip Sheridan, hero of the Civil War. The sculpture, rising above the intersection, depicts General Sheridan, mounted on a rearing horse, in combat.

And every spring Mike Krukow supervises the painting of the horse's balls.

Before Krukow, there were others. It's a baseball tradition.

Every team bus driver, you see, takes the same route from downtown Chicago to Wrigley Field and every time a bus passes the statue, somebody invariably shouts, "Don't look at the horse's balls, it'll bring you bad luck."

Or, if things have not been going well, somebody might say, "Look at the horse's balls and it'll change your luck!"

And every spring, somebody paints the horse's balls. Sometimes, in one summer that horse will take on several coats of paint. And that brings us back to Krukow, a 20-game winner for the Giants in 1986. Every year when the Giants make their first visit to Chicago, Mike cons some rookies into painting the horse's testicles, assuring them that the local police are aware of the tradition and would never dream of arresting anyone. Right.

Last season Krukow got even more ambitious.

"It was a regular raid," he said. "We had seven rookies attacking in two separate skirmishes (the painters missed a spot the first time)."

There was even a San Francisco television crew on hand to record the decorating of the General's steed.

"But maybe that wasn't such a good idea," said Krukow. "Al Rosen (Giants' exec) saw his players crawling all over a statue on TV and didn't think it was so funny. He took me to the shed."

Does anybody want to wager on whether Krukow's Raiders will strike again during the spring or summer of 1987?

After all, aren't ballplayers under enough pressure on the field of play? Can't boys be boys even if they are old enough to be men?

Sometimes I wonder if athletes in other sports shouldn't loosen up a little. Do you ever hear about a professional golfer pulling a practical joke? Is the pressure of competing on a pro golf tour so great on an individual that there simply isn't room for silliness?

Terry Forster, my ex-teammate with the White Sox and successful left-handed relief pitcher in both leagues during the past 17 years, told me about attending the Los Angeles Open as a spectator:

Terry was standing behind the green talking to a buddy when golfer Curtis Strange turns around and says, "Sssshhhhhhhh."

Forster responded as any red-blooded baseball player would.

"Why don't you stick that putter up your ass?" asked Terry, and before he could frame a second question, he was being ejected from the golf course by security men.

That, to me, is amazing but typical. Baseball players are subjected to every distraction from knives to cowbells, and a pro golfer can't handle the click of a camera? It's so ridiculous that even the announcers at golf tournaments whisper.

Want a good example? Before striking a shot in the Atlanta Golf Classic last summer, this is what pro Bob Tway did to get ready—according to a description in the *Atlanta Journal-Constitution*:

> He took off his glove, adjusted his visor, hitched up his pants, looked at his yardage book, made a phantom swing, stood with hands on hips looking down the fairway, flicked grass off his slacks, dried his club grips with a towel, took counsel with his caddy, made another phantom swing, rechecked the yardage book, slipped his glove on (working each finger in precisely, as a surgeon might), selected a club, said something to his caddy, made a practice swing with the club, moved alongside the ball, raised his right hand off the club and reapplied it, waggled the clubhead over the ball, turned his head to look down the line of the shot, turned back to the ball, looked

down the line a second time, and then decided he had the wrong club. He started over.

Started over?

I've got an even better starting over story: It's midnight and raining outside Jack Murphy Stadium, San Diego. Three sportswriters, finished with deadlines, walk into the parking lot to the small rental car being driven by Kevin Modesti of the *Los Angeles Daily News*. Destination, L.A.

One of the writers gets into the passenger's seat and tries to figure out the radio. Modesti, meanwhile, is trying to figure out how to work the windshield wipers. The third man, 260-pound Matt (Bags) McHale of the *Pasadena Star-News*, will sit in the back seat.

The back door slams. Modesti gets the windshield wiper going, and says to his passenger riding shotgun:

"How do we get out of this place? Which gate is open?"

So they maneuver through the parking lot, find Friars Road through the rain and darkness, and even find a country & western music station on the radio.

They've gone about five miles when Modesti says:

"You're awfully quiet back there, Matt."

They go another mile and the other passenger says: "Hey, Matt, you fall asleep already?

"Matt? Are you there, Matt?"

But Matt isn't there. Somehow, 260-pound Matt isn't there.

"How can this be?" asked Modesti. "Didn't you hear him get into the car?"

"I heard him."

"Then where is he?"

So they turn around, drive six miles back, enter the

Jack Murphy Stadium parking lot, and there sits McHale, in the rain, under a tree.

"What happened?" asked Modesti.

"I opened the door, tossed in my computer, closed the door, and turned around to take a leak," said Matt. "That's when you drove off."

"Why didn't you yell at us?"

"I thought you were kidding."

They started over.

It would seem, then, that baseball players aren't the only ones to occasionally behave erratically.

It is a sport, however, which over the years has produced some chuckles.

Over the edge?

Norm Cash once went to the plate carrying a piano leg instead of a bat to hit against Nolan Ryan.

Steve Yeager went on the Rev. Robert Schuller's TV show to heal his sore knee and it worked.

Al Campanis, vice president of the Dodgers, once told a minor leaguer to hit four ground balls, then run to second as fast as he could. The kid hit four grounders and ran directly over the pitcher's mount to second.

Campanis also sold his own son, Jimmy, to the Kansas City organization for $100,000. And, said Al to Jimmy later: "Son, if I'd known how much weight you were going to gain, I'd have sold you by the pound."

Organist Helen Dell played "Charge!" before a game at Dodger Stadium one night and every pitcher, led by Jerry Reuss, galloped out of the dugout, took a hard left at third base, and raced to the bullpen.

Bill Madlock brought a 400-pound fan out of the stands, dressed him in Mike Scioscia's uniform shirt, and put him in the cage for batting practice.

Reggie Jackson got so upset one night in Cleveland that he broke every light bulb in the tunnel leading from the dugout to the clubhouse. The rest of the Yankees returned in darkness.

When retired and overweight Willie Stargell showed up in Atlanta to coach, somebody in the Braves' clubhouse suggested they get a couple of drive-in movie screens to make him some uniform pants.

Johnny Logan ran eight times for county sheriff in Milwaukee and lost every time. Said Johnny: "But it only cost me $500."

Ryne Duren says the most accurate pitch he ever made was into the stands in Denver. He hit a heckler in the stomach and got a two-game suspension.

Cleveland pitcher Phil Niekro, wearing a red mask, charged out of the dugout during a 1986 game, dived into second base headfirst, then sprinted back into the dugout while stunned umpire Dave Phillips gave the safe sign.

Over the edge? Bill Lee once said: "It's a scientific fact that the left side of your brain controls the right side of your body, and the right side of your brain controls the left side of your body. Therefore, left-handers are the only people in their right mind."

Joe Charboneau fixed his own broken nose with pliers.

Frank Thomas once shoved winter ball teammate Sad Sam Jones into a swimming pool, but after discovering he couldn't swim, jumped in to save him. Three years later, Thomas homered off Jones and Sad Sam got so mad he wouldn't speak to him.

"What's the matter?" asked Thomas.

"Christ, you hit a dinger off me," lamented Jones. "You cost me the game."

"I saved your life, you son of a bitch," said Thomas. "I should have let you drown."

Jimmy Stewart, one of my ex-teammates with the Angels, now works for Kansas City, and said about scouting Bo Jackson:

"I saw him hit a ball 550 feet in high school."

"So what?" I said. "A lot of guys can hit the ball that far."

"Yeah," said Jimmy, "but how many can then run out and catch it?"

Ted Williams would take a .22 rifle to Fenway Park before batting practice and shoot pigeons out of the light standards.

Reggie Jax once gave a dugout water cooler six karate chops, lifted it, and threw it onto the field.

Lou Piniella showed up for a spring training game in 1978 without his shoes, size 9½, so he borrowed a pair of size 10s from teammate Thurman Munson. About the third inning, though, Piniella sat down, took off the shoes, and threw them over the outfield fence. "They didn't fit," said Piniella.

Gene Freese went over the edge one night in Cincinnati when, after unsuccessfully chasing a fly ball, he continued running through the outfield scoreboard door and got lost inside.

Dave Kingman sent a live rat into the press box addressed to: "Sue Fornoff, Sac Bee." "He couldn't spell Sacramento," said sportswriter Fornoff.

Phillie manager Danny Ozark once put a batting ring on the end of a skinny fungo bat, took a swing, and the metal ring flew off and hit pitcher Randy Lerch in the middle of the forehead.

Then there was the time Ozark started to the

mound to relieve Wayne Twitchell, but slipped on the last dugout step and fell flat. Embarrassed, he immediately returned to his seat and watched Twitchell give up three more runs.

My buddy Bill Melton established a major league record with 12 consecutive strikeouts in 1970 and got a standing ovation from the press box. "When the fans started cheering me for foul tips," says Melton, "I decided it was time to go catch a cab."

Then there was the night Yogi Berra went 4 for 4, but picked up the box score the next day and saw he was credited with only 3 for 4. So he showed the official scorer the box score, and said, "What's going on?"

"Oh," said the apologetic scorer, "don't worry about that. It's a typographical error."

"Bullshit!" said Yogi. "It was a clean hit up the middle."

You don't believe all those Yogi Berra stories? How about this one: He came home after a rained-out game and nobody was home. So he sat around the house for about four hours, watching TV and getting irritated. Then his wife, Carmen, walks through the door:

"Where in hell were you?"

"I took the kid to see *Dr. Zhivago,*" she said.

"What the heck is wrong with him now?"

And every time I think working for a radio or television station might be okay, I'm reminded of this incident involving Larry Kahn, sports announcer for radio station KNX in Los Angeles.

Kahn kept leading with the Len Bias story, every 15 minutes with something new. But then he got a call from the news director.

"Why are you hitting the story so hard?" he asked.

"Because it's the biggest story in sports," said Kahn.

"Christ," said the news director, "he's already been dead for three hours."

Then there was sportswriter Peter Schmuck of the *Orange County Register*; yes, the same Schmuck who put a crab in the bed of Angels' relief pitcher Donnie Moore, the same Schmuck who got so weary of explaining that Peter Schmuck was really his name that he ordered a personalized California license plate which read: SCHMUCK.

Somebody stole it.

In some of my likes and dislikes about the game today, I'm in the minority: I like the designated hitter, domed stadiums, and artificial turf.

15
THE GAME

My first major league hit, in 1966, came off Gary Bell. My last one, September 1985, 20 seasons later, was the game winner against Montreal, a base hit in the bottom of the 12th to win a game the Dodgers needed during a pennant race.

Looking back, I can't blame my old buddy Bob Rodgers for not having me walked that night with first base open. I couldn't even blame him the next day when he spotted me walking across the field and said, "Fuck you. I should have known better."

That was one of the nicest things he could have said to me. It was a long major league ride, from the mid-sixties to the mid-eighties. I go back with Rodgers to those early days with the Angels.

And things sure have changed since then. I don't want to sound like one of those old-timers who are always griping how the game of baseball has gone to hell. But like everything else, baseball has indeed changed.

Television, for example. Does TV have impact or what? I've been hosting interview shows on the West Coast and it seems like more people recognize me now than when I played. And I'm not even wearing my umbrella hat anymore. Sports fans depend so much on TV that sometimes I wonder how we got along without it (but every time I say that, I'm reminded by sportswriters that it wasn't so bad).

Example of impact: during a 17–14 loss to the New York Giants during the 1986 pro football season, offensive tackle Phil Pozderac of the Dallas Cowboys made three critical errors. The next day, *Dallas Morning News* columnist David Casstevens, describing Pozderac's sins, wrote: "For those of you who have been calling, the public flogging will be noon on Wednesday."

The next day somebody called the newspaper sports department and asked: "Will it be televised?"

I've even been fooling with the entertainment world between playing in Old-Timers Games and running an auto parts business. But, hey, that's not so easy either. I did a bit part as an announcer in the movie *Body Slam* with the Lakers' announcer Chick Hearn, and a 280-pound pro wrestler named Captain Lou knocked me off my chair. Where does the script say "Pro wrestler lands in ex-baseball player's lap"?

Before getting too carried away with future endeavors, though, I would like to leave you with some observations about the state of my game, baseball.

Other than the uncertainty of drug testing, and rumors about collusion among owners against paying huge salaries to free agents, the players of today have few reasons for complaint. It has become a player's game.

If I had the power, though, there *are* a few slight changes I would make:

I'd shorten the season and lengthen spring training.

This is not necessarily because the greatest pranks of all time have occurred during spring training, although it is something to think about. No, I'd shorten the season because nobody needs 162 games, certainly not the players or fans and not even the owners, if they would admit it. Shorten the season to 154 games, as it used to be, and performances would rise.

I think teams rush into exhibition games in spring training without giving players enough time for preparation. You can't get ready in 10 days. Yet, perhaps because they don't want to pay the extra money, owners won't let players report until March 1. I think a player should be allowed to go to spring training earlier if he wishes. And the owners' argument that "you should be in shape before you get there" doesn't wash. Getting into shape is what spring training is supposed to be about—not the playing of extra exhibition games so the owners can make money to defray costs.

In some likes and dislikes about the game today, I'm in the minority: I like the designated hitter, domed stadiums, and artificial turf.

I especially like the DH if you're going to have 24-man rosters. National League teams last season ran so short of players, they were using pitchers as pinch hitters. I saw some pitchers playing outfield. Frankly, I think the fans want more action—hits, runs, and even errors.

Domed stadiums make sense, especially in cold-weather cities. And if Florida ever expects to have major league baseball, which it deserves, promoters there had better start talking about domed stadiums. Climate can be controlled indoors and playing conditions are ideal.

Also, just in case you thought I was being totally objective, indoors is better for the hitters, and isn't that what baseball is all about—hitting the ball?

Some things, however, do bother me about the game today: Where are the superstars? Where are the power hitters? Who are the tough guys?

I don't see superstars anymore in the National League. They're all in the American League. Who's going to fill the shoes of Stan Musial, Willie Mays, Ernie Banks, Willie Stargell, Henry Aaron, Roberto Clemente, Bob Gibson, or Sandy Koufax? The closest thing to a pitching superstar in the NL is Fernando Valenzuela, who hasn't missed a start in six seasons. Then, there's Steve Garvey, Mike Schmidt, and Dale Murphy—but Schmidt and Garv are nearing the ends of their careers, and if Murphy is a legit superstar, shouldn't he be hitting 45 home runs every year in that Atlanta ballpark?

I love the National League, but the pendulum is swinging the other way. What great rookies have come up recently in the N.L.? Maybe it's just a trend but I think the owners should start paying attention to the way that the great youngsters are going.

Not enough hitters are hitting 30 or more home runs. Not anymore. Nowadays if you hit 20 homers, you're a slugging hero.

Why? Relief pitching and the split-fingered fastball, that's why. It's an age of specialization, and great relief pitching has taken a toll on batting averages and home-run production. And the split-fingered pitch is the toughest adjustment for hitters since the slider came into being. Against a great one like Bruce Sutter, who started this split-fingered landslide, you could at least step forward in the batter's box because he couldn't get the fastball past you.

Now, though, there are pitchers throwing 92 miles an hour and still making it fall off the table. Step up on them and the ball goes past you. They're throwing pitches that look like fastballs but drop straight down, right through the strike zone.

Finally, the rare bird of major league baseball is the man who plays 162 games. Even more rare is the man who *wants* to play 162 games.

At one time there was an unspoken understanding among quality players: "Even if I'm hurt, I can still play better than the guy behind me, and therefore I can help my team more than he can."

A lot of players don't feel that way anymore, and I don't understand it. Maybe it's the money, maybe the multi-year, guaranteed contracts. But it *has* hurt the game. There are players now who think nothing of playing three days in a row, then asking for a day off, even if they have no injuries. They just figure they need a day of rest to "keep themselves strong."

I think it's a joke. Teams nowadays have strength coaches, assistant trainers, assistant team doctors, dietitians, stretching experts, psychologists, dentists, and physical therapists.

They also have more people on the disabled list than at any time in the history of baseball.

The above comment, incidentally, may sound a little hypocritical when you consider that I spent most of my final season on the DL. Some of the L.A. writers, in fact, were sure I was just being "carried" on the roster by Lasorda.

Actually, I had an inflamed hip socket—originally hurt in 1984 with the Cubs when diving for a ball—then aggravated early in 1985 when I stepped on a sprinkler head in the outfield. Perhaps if I'd been 18 or 28 it wouldn't have taken so long to heal. As it was, at the age of 38 I could hardly run during that final season.

I was talking about it just the other day, in fact, with a Beverly Hills psychologist.

Psychologist? Hmmm. I can hear my former teammates and managers thudding to the floor from shock. How long have those guys been trying to get me into a straitjacket? Well, this psychologist came without his butterfly net. He just wanted to know if I had been psychologically affected by my hip injury.

I told him yes, that I worried about someday not being able to play in Old-Timers Games without falling down.

Then I asked him if there were any problems I could solve for him, and the conversation deteriorated from there.

I was kind of disappointed. After all, the mental health profession and I go back a long way, from the days in high school when we used to raid the nearby state mental hospital to more recent years when some of my teammates tried to have me elected Mental Health Poster Child.

Maybe Jerry Reuss was wrong. Maybe I'm not just a product of my environment. Maybe I've always been this way. It's been a long time since that hit off of Gary Bell in 1966, and a lot of things have changed in this sport. But one thing has always remained the same—the way I feel about this little boy's game. When you're standing at the plate, it's sometimes hard to remember whether you're fourteen or forty.

For the historians: in my last regular-season at-bat as a major league baseball player, on the final day of the 1985 season, I tried to beat out a grounder to shortstop and executed a perfect belly-flop slide across first base. The TV replay showed I was safe but the ump called me out anyhow, and I figured that was as good a way to end a career as any.

I played 30 years of organized baseball, from my first Little League game at age nine to the day Jack Clark homered off Tom Niedenfuer to eliminate the Dodgers from the 1985 National League playoffs.

During the 1986 season, however, I saw baseball from a different perspective.

Boy, it sure looks easy from the press box.

I heard myself saying things like, "How can that guy not get that ball?" or, "That's an error," before realizing what I should not have forgotten:

It isn't as easy as it looks, folks.

Those men, young and old, playing major league baseball are an elite few, 644 out of four billion people in the world. Fair criticism is important, but so is insight and humor.

Especially humor.

You've gotta have it. Believe me, you don't last in baseball without it. If you turn every strikeout or loss into a life-or-death situation, you'll never be around to collect the hits and wins.

This may come as a surprise to some baseball die-hards, but there *is* a game that's more important than the one being played in the ballparks. It's called *life*. It's living, caring, giving, loving—enjoying what we have and making the most out of every minute. Life's too short to worry about every error, pop-up, and foul ball. And if you can't cope with the battles within the white lines, how are you going to deal with real life? If you can't keep your chin up after a loss, how are you going to deal with a *real* crisis?

Ballplayers are idolized by millions of fans (well, in my case there are probably only six or seven, including Daryl Brilliant), but I've seen those who take the game so seriously that they have no life outside baseball. Their reality is the game. And I just want to tell them, hey guys, it *is* a pretty great game, but it is *only* a game. The applause, the glory—it all means nothing unless you can leave the stadium and share it with people you care about and who care about you. Your friends, your family, your kids.

Kids. I have the world's most beautiful daughter, Mary Jayne Sarah, who is six, and I wish I could figure out how she got to be so old. I suppose when you play baseball you miss out on a few things. But if I can teach her a little of what I've learned over the years about people and life (and maybe even something about how to hit a slider), maybe we can make up for lost time.

One final message, too, for those young people who dream about someday becoming a big league ballplayer:

Set your goals high and reach.

You must believe in yourself no matter how many times you fail, no matter what people tell you, because you can prove them wrong through hard work, determination, and practice.

If you want something badly enough and believe in it, you'll be surprised at the strength you will find within yourself.

Never give up. I think it was the late Vince Lombardi, coach of the Green Bay Packers, who said: "I never lost a game. I just ran out of time."

So now that I've finally taken off that uniform after 22 years, I know that the game of life is the *only* game I'll be playing from now on.

And I can't wait.

ACKNOWLEDGMENTS

Special thanks to everyone who laughed with me about the stories in this book: Joey Amalfitano, Jerry Reuss, Al Hrabosky, Steve Sax, Orlando Cepeda, Gaylord Perry, Peter Schmuck, Davey Johnson, Roger Repoz, Clyde Wright, Richie Scheinblum, Alan Meersand, Al Campanis, Mike Krukow, Terry Forster, Johnny Logan, Frank Thomas, Jimmy Stewart, Bill Melton, Tom Egan, Larry Kahn, Jon Scott, Mitch Poole, Stu Nahan, Ken Swofford, Jim (Mudcat) Grant, Joe Pignatano, Bruce Froemming, Dutch (Pee Wee) Rennert, Eric Gregg, Charlie Williams, Steve Garvey, Dan Driessen, Hoyt Wilhelm, Luke Appling, Bill (Moose) Skowron, Stan Williams, Dick Groat, Kent Tekulve, Joe Torre, Jim O'Toole, Charlie Hough, Bobby Valentine, Pat Corrales, Chris Speier, Bill DeLury, Bobby Wine, Mike Schmidt, Tom Paciorek, Richie Ashburn, Brant Alyea, Albie Pearson, Jim Fregosi, Tom Grimes, Steve Yeager, Gene Michael,

Bob Gibson, Bill Russell, Mrs. Marion Peterson, Bob (Chopper) Hunter, Jody Davis, Lee Elia, Daryl Brilliant, Andy Carbone, Joe McDonnell, Richard (Itchy) Jones, Nancy Mazmanian, Marc Dellins, Ron Fairly, Lou Pavlovich, Jr., Leslie Jackman, Bruce Levine, Gordon Verrell, Terry Johnson, Kevin Modesti, Randy Youngman, Matt McHale, and Mary Jayne Johnstone.

Also, my deepest gratitude to those special friends who helped me see that it wasn't so hard to make the transition from baseball player to mere mortal: Tom Lasorda, who has always treated me like a son; Ron Masak, a great actor whose own sense of humor always makes me laugh; the Los Angeles Dodgers, who have given me the honor of playing on their community service team; Al Campanis, who lets me watch games with him in his private box in Dodger Stadium and gives me a better perspective of the game; Mark Brunett, who never lost faith in me; Chuck Friedman and the gang at Sportswide Productions, who have started me on a whole new career; Mike Roarty and all my good friends at Anheuser-Busch; John Stoll of Delta Airlines and Dick Jennings at American Airlines, who have made all the miles I travel much more pleasant; Bill Reigert, the former Angel and my good friend in Florida who stands by me and is always ready to pick up my pieces in case I fall off the wall; Joe Masino, who does such a great job running my charity softball tournaments; Chuck Poehler of Goodman's Sporting Goods and Richard Maertz of All-American Sporting Goods, who have donated so much to the softball tournaments; and my good friends in the produce houses of Los Angeles— Charlie, Jack, Corky, and Poochie—who have lent a hand as well; Harry and Gary Hindoyan of Burger

Continental in Pasadena, who are always there for me; Jimmy Filipan of Stevens Steakhouse; Tony at the Market Restaurant; Tommy's good friend Larry at Paul's Kitchen; Lou and his brothers at Trani's in San Pedro; my newfound friends in the city of El Monte, who have helped me with my auto parts store; and Roy Webb, my new partner who has turned my business around and put me on the right track.

And finally, to all the baseball fans across the country: I hope I've given you as many great moments as you've given me.